ENCYCLOPEDIA
CORRUPTION
IN THE WORLD

Book 3: Legal Perspective of Corruption

JUDIVAN J. VIEIRA

authorHOUSE®

AuthorHouse™
1663 Liberty Drive
Bloomington, IN 47403
www.authorhouse.com
Phone: 1 (800) 839-8640

Published by AuthorHouse 11/15/2018

ISBN: 978-1-5462-5508-6 (sc)
ISBN: 978-1-5462-5506-2 (hc)
ISBN: 978-1-5462-5507-9 (e)

Library of Congress Control Number: 2018909723

Thanks to:

My mother (in memoriam), who told me when I was still the assistant of a bricklayer that studying would make a difference in my life.

Eliane Caetano, advisor and head of my personal office for efficiency and help in the research phase and bibliographic organization, during the five years that made this work a scientific reality and an innovative proposal.

Neither the corrupt nor the virtuous has power over their moral behavior, but they had, rather, power to become one thing or another; so also someone who throws a stone has power over it before hurling it, but does not have it after having thrown it.

Aristotle

CONTENTS

Introduction...xiii

Legal Perspective of Corruption xv

Chapter 1   Of the Legal Norms 1

    1.1 - Characteristics of legal rules.. 9

    1.2 - Logical structure of the moral norm and legal norm 10

    1.2.1 - Logical structure of the moral norm 10

    1.2.2 - Logical structure of the legal norm 12

    1.3 - Categorical norms and hypothetical norms.....................13

    1.4 - Validity of the legal system 14

    1.5 - The right to resist any unjust norm of positive law 20

Chapter 2   Anti-Corruption Criminal Law in Mercosur.................... 24

Chapter 3   Some Proofs of Simmetry among the Jurisprudence
             of Mercosur...31

    3.1 - Argentina 32

    3.2 - Brazil - (conviction for embezzlement) 33

    3.3 - Paraguay (open case) 34

    3.4 - About Venezuela... 34

Chapter 4   Internal Legal Order of Combat of Corruption 38

    4.1 - Table - Organic Laws of the Mercosur Public
          Administrations..41

Chapter 5   Legislation on Ethics in Mercosur.................................... 46

5.1 - Centrifugal corruption and centripetal corruption 49

5.2 - The vision of International Law on Ethics 49

5.3 - The view of Mercosul Legal Systems on ethics 60

5.4 - Code of ethics of the public function - Argentina............. 63

5.5 - Brazilian legislation on ethics in Federal Public
       Administration (Inpired on The Inter-American
       Convention Against Corruption(IACAC) 65

5.6 – Code of ethics of the public function / Paraguay............. 68

5.7 - Legislation on ethics in the public service in Uruguay 69

5.8 - Legislation on ethics in the public service in
       Venezuela - Decree 41/9.. 70

Chapter 6   White Collar Crimes - An International Concern............. 73

6.1 - Concept of white collar crime 75

6.2 - Pillars or Grounds of White Collar Crime 77

6.3 - The protected legal object guarded by law in white-
       collar crime 77

6.4 - White collar crime relationship with corruption.............. 78

6.5 - White collar crimes legislation in Mercosur Public
       Administrations...81

Chapter 7   Existence of Law against Corruption in the
             Mercosur, afert Approval of the Inter-American
             Convention Against Corruption - IACAC 102

7.1 - Comparative tables of Mercosur member countries,
       on specific law to combat corruption..............................103

Chapter 8   Laws of Public Administrations of Mercosur 110

Chapter 9   Symmetries of the Extraterritorial Crimes against
             the Public Administrations of Mercosur 128

9.1 - Table on symmetries of the principle of territoriality
       in Mercosur Criminal Law 129

9.2 - Table of symmetries in extraterritorial crimes
    against the Mercosur Public Administrations - MPA.......134

9.3 - Brazilian law that amends the Criminal Code and
    promotes the liability of a natural person who
    commits an act of corruption against foreign public
    administration 159

9.4 - New Brazilian law that provides for the
    administrative and civil liability of legal
    persons for the practice of acts against public
    administration, national or foreign 161

9.4.1 - Message of the vetoes by the President of Brazil,
    as an extrajudicial element of interpretation of the
    law N°. 12,846 / 2013:..178

9.4.2 - Comments on Law no. 12.846 / 2013............................180

Chapter 10   Process System for Legal Assessment of Public
    Functional Resources in Mercosur..................................190

10.1 - Specific procedure for the prosecution of crimes
    of civil servants 192

10.2 - the rules of the Brazilian common procedure 201

Final Considerations on the Book III.. 203
Author's Comments... 207
Bibliography...211

INTRODUCTION

Two political philosophies struggle with greater visibility in the world. the political-anarchist philosophy that proclaims the total absence of the state and its consecrative, such as power, laws, hierarchy and domination, and the political-juridical philosophy adopted in democratic states of law, whose values are exactly the opposite of anarchism.

This work embraces the political-legal philosophy, but disconcerted that the ruling class is making a supernatural effort to prove that the formula is not effective.

How does the right see corruption? if law as a social science has the comprehensive role of building, interpreting, and helping to govern life in society, what degree of commitment do I attribute to corruption as a disaggregating factor? How do you sanction the conduct of the corrupt?

There are many questions that can be asked about the legal perspective of corruption.

It is true that no other science has so many arguments and tools to combat this human malady.

The greatest of all questions, however, is whether the legislator and the enforcer of law are willing to be ethical and moral and to sacrifice their personal interests for the common good.

I hope that the reflections that follow inspire the ethical ideal and rekindle the fire that still remains in the few embers of the bonfire of those who believe that this formal justice can become substantial justice.

Judivan Vieira

LEGAL PERSPECTIVE OF CORRUPTION

Law from the last two centuries has been transforming into a fantastic dream factory. A kind of Disney. The contours of what he draws are beautiful, but what he draws is not effective.

It is infinitely greater the number of promises contained in unreal or real laws (some inapplicable) than the material realization of social welfare, which the Liberal state promises us by its formal Constitutions.

Law has learned much more from politics than the politics with law, which is why formal democracy is reality and substantive democracy is an eternal promise.

The law is being lost in the course of its historical journey. It has been transformed into cold lyrics, in mere literal science. He has slowly sold his soul to the "devil" and sub-serenely bowed before the political sphere as a mere instrument of support for his shadowy interests, rather than a steady step toward justice.

I agree with Jerônimo Jesus Santos (2005: 56) when he says that law, without the concern for access to justice, does not have the irreplaceable commitment to reality.

However, it is not our intention in this work to confuse access to justice with actions or procedural remedies, because access to justice even exists. It is a path full of thorns, but it exists! the greatest of problems is that at the end of the twisting journey, justice is not.

We propose justice as the conception of the "just", the supreme Good, believing that only his inspiration can lead governments to understand that the people will wake up and see that the democracies we have today are merely formal and, there will be no escape from the right of resistance, foreseen in the 1776 declaration of victory and political-juridical institutes, like impeachment, foreseen in constitutions of the states of law.

The state needs to review the position of mere supporter conferred on the right and try to fulfill its desideratum of effecting a justice that substantively gives the people the counterpart to their tributary efforts and fidelity to the principle of domination, to promote justice that confers dignity, a corollary of substantial democracy, as inferred, for example, from the promise in art. 6 of the Brazilian constitution of 1988, which says:

"Social rights are education, health, food, work, housing, leisure, security, social security, protection of motherhood and childhood, assistance to the destitute, in the form of this constitution. (wording given by Constitutional Amendment No. 64 of 2010)"

The question to be asked to mens legislators is: When will social rights be made available to society in a substantial way?

The legal model adopted by our formal democracies demonstrates that politics and law have joined the art of ruling by promises. In this chapter we will continue to address corruption with public goods, monies, and incomes, and now, from a legal standpoint.

We will note the existence of good laws of combat to the corruption in all the countries-members of the Mercosur, will study the structure of the moral standard and of the legal standard, for to the end to be still convinced of what there are efficient legal instruments to reduce the corruption and to make the social rights effective, as promised by democratic Constitutions.

CHAPTER I

Of the Legal Norms

Alain Supiot in an excellent work on Homo Juridicus reaffirms the eternal dichotomy between of being and of that of being-must. In this two-way intellectual walk, it is certain that the law is not divine, but human (something that the pre-Socratics already said in the fifth century BC) and its norms, as such, exist to govern conflicting human relations. this is what Supiot says:

"The profound error and basic unrealism of jurists who think it realistic to eliminate considerations of justice in the analysis of law is to forget that man is a two-dimensional being whose social life is developed on the ground of being and of that of being-must. the law is not revealed by God nor discovered by science, it is a fully human work in which those who study it participate and who can not interpret it without taking into account the values it conveys."

The law aims to promote justice through its norms, principles and decisions. Norms can be moral or legal.

The legal norms are substrate of a right that in our feeling is of three natures: volatile, floating and seasonal.

1– Volatile: because it shows inconstancy in his convictions. It almost always gives up its power space to politics;
2– Floating: because it is applied according to political convenience. The Law can hardly ever stand on its own. the strength of its norms does not overlap with political will even when it is not focused on social justice; and

1

3– Seasonal: because applied according to the government of the moment, as happened with Hitler's National Socialism(Fascism with a different name), Mussolini's Fascism, Soviet Communism, exception regimes and capitalist civilian governments uncommitted with social welfare.

Morally there is no difference between such governments when they relegate the probity and well-being of the people to the background and assume that their personal interests justify the impoverishment of the nation.

The dominant classes create the ideology that favors them, invent wills and affections that induce man to think as he interests them.

The social consciousness is born of the dominant intellect and gradually becomes the unconscious of the dominated, when it becomes a mere useful instrument to the masters of Power.

The State of Law is a social institution subservient to the ruling class that is masterly able to use the fallacy as foundation of law and its formal rights.

The man is inclined to take for truth what is useful to him. Francis Bacon addresses this truth as follows:

"The human intellect is not pure light, because it receives influence from the will and from the affections, from which it is possible to generate the science that is wanted. For man is inclined to take as truth what he prefers. in view of this, rejects the difficulties, driven by the impatience of research; the sobriety, because he suffered hope; the supreme principles of nature, in favor of superstition; the light of experience, in favor of arrogance and pride, avoiding seeming to deal with vile and ephemeral things; paradoxes, out of respect for the opinion of the people. In short, innumerable are the formulas by which feeling, almost always imperceptibly, insinuates itself and affects the intellect."

Legal positivism and its reductionism have already conditioned our concept of justice to normative truth, different from the jusnaturalist thought for which justice, as opposed to positive law, is not and should not be manipulated.

The right rule always seeks the most valuable conduct, as emphasized by the Professor Inmério Jorge Catenacci :

"The moral norm positively states morally valuable behavior. The legal norm, on the other hand, generally states the conduct to which the legal consequence will be imputed, that is to say, it establishes the unlawful act or conduct that is legally reproached."

Thomas Hobbes remains alive in his words about the good law and the bad law and explains in a crystalline way the differences between the two:

"It belongs to the sovereign's care to make good laws. But what is a good law? By good law I mean only a just law, for no law can be unjust. the law is made by the sovereign power and all that is made by such power is guaranteed and concerns the whole people, and whatever a man has, no one can say that it is unjust. (...) Unnecessary laws are not good laws, but traps for money, which are superfluous when the sovereign's right is recognized, and when it is not recognized they are insufficient to defend the people."

Those who are not inclined to think are easy prey to those who know how to master and manipulate.

The great mass of the people is induced to superstition, because to investigate and to believe scientifically is the privilege of the few. The population mass can not overcome the phase of dogmas and this is of interest to those who dominate, since controlling a thinking mass requires negotiating and sharing social welfare more equitably, which for the political classes means loss of power, which is why always show themselves reticent to the promotion of isonomy.

Hobbes's lucidity continues to inspire other who agree that the law will not necessarily be fair just because it is a law, as it says Eduardo Morón Alcain:

"Legal positivism and the separation between law and morality," in which in other respects it refers to the right that is and to the right that must be, and that "the truly liberal response ... (is that) law is not morality; (...) Laws can be right even if they are too bad to be obeyed"

It is a fact that positivism is not the only conditioning circumstance of law, because as affirmed doctor Ruppert F. J. Pritzl, the political system, of all, is the greatest manipulator. Behold in his words:

"... in less democratic countries ... laws and official dispositions must always be analyzed according to the political system ..."

When politics assumes the role of conditioner of the law, and this occurs frequently in all regimes of government, what is seen is a servile and servile right.

Noam Chomsky was not mistaken about the damages of a subservient right:

"I do not know concrete and substantive programs to promote social change that is extremely necessary and technically feasible. the political system offers few possibilities. (...) the Ministry seeks to show that Proudhon was right in writing that the laws are "spider webs for the rich and powerful, chains that no steel is capable of breaking for the small and weak, and fishing nets in the hands of the government."

Manuel Hespanha in tracing the historical profile of law from its codification to the moral content of its norms states:

"Finally, the idea of bringing laws together in systematic and enduring codes also corresponded to this idea of the "hull of law", which was now codified as the normative, perennial and consensual nucleus of life in society.

Statualism (i.e., identification of the social order with the state order), certainty and predictability of law (i.e., abstract legislation), and finally, the fixity and permanence of a fundamental nucleus of legal principles (i.e., codification), they walk arm in arm to provide effectiveness and stabilization of the new social, political and juridical arrangements.

The hundred years between 1750 and 1850 correspond to the period of installation of a new political and juridical order, which is often called liberalism. At the law level, its strategic assumptions are then made - by legislative means, a new paradigm of political organization (the liberal-representative state) and of social organization ("proprietary liberalism", ie, identification of property as a condition of freedom and thus of active citizenship), which the law itself will develop in its institutional details (...)

The "critique of law"

The first aspect leads to a new concern to understand how law creates systems of classification and hierarchy, norms and images, which condition or even institute power relationships in society. these are the schools of "critique du droit" (critique du droit, critical legal studies, Rechtskritik), which have developed mainly in France, the United States and Germany since the mid-1970s.

Although the movements of the 'critique of law' - especially in France - have depended heavily on the Marxist critique of law, one can find for them a more specific inspiration in the thinking of the Frankfurt school which in the 1960s undertook a disassembly quite systematically from the ideological assumptions of culture (understood in its broadest sense, from music to common sense) of the Western world. (...)

All these levels of production of power are conceived as cultural artifacts, i.e. as the product of a "local" organization (or "construction") of social reality carried out by social groups at a certain historical moment.

Law is also the result of an arbitrary, local, historical production of social groups. But, in addition, it is also an instrument for constructing representations (the subject of law, contract, property, state), categories (the madman, the criminal, the woman, the black) and the corresponding social hierarchies.

The function of the critique of law is, on the one hand, to uncover the social unthinking ones that are at the root of legal representations, demystifying the points of view that law is a rational, neutral and objectively founded order in social reality (i.e., in the nature of things).

"The apogee of formalism. The pure theory of law"

Kelsen considered law as a special system of norms, the basis of which was not in other normative systems, such as religion or morals; but it was also not in the order of events (for example, in politics, in utility). That is, a legal rule would not be effective because it is moral or useful, but because it is only because it is a legal norm, i.e., according to the law. to be in conformity with the law is, after all, to be obligatory by virtue of the command of a higher standard. Hence the law constitutes a normative pyramid (Stufen theory), on top of which is the Constitution. But since the Constitution itself lacks a legal basis, Kelsen's theoretical construction presupposes a "fundamental norm" (Grundnorm), which validates the Constitution, and whose content could be formulated as such - "the entire legal norm of law (ie, established according to law) must be observed ". A norm of these is self-referential, that is, it applies to itself; and thereby legitimates itself and all others.

The pure theory of law had the virtue, in a period of intense politicalideological debate (1930s to 1950s), to have underlined the autonomy of legal knowledge and its relative unavailability in relation to the projects of power. To that extent, it has culminated the concerns of pandects in stating that not everything that is wanted by power, useful to the people or to a class, or functional in relation to a social goal, is automatically accepted as fair (i.e., according to the right). Juridicity seems to flow from internal values to the discourse of law, values that political will or social utility can not replace.

In this sense, although the pure theory of the right to accept as law everything that comes from the will of the state can be accused, its deeper meaning is to constitute a manifesto against the political totalitarianisms of its time, which in one direction or another sought to functionalize law in relation to the conveniences of power, legitimizing it from political considerations such as class domination (Stalinism) or the vital needs of a race (National Socialism). There are those who think that this manifesto is still useful against other types of functionalization of the law, namely, the tendency to justify as fair the measures - formally or informally correct - of a power legitimized by voting, or measures directed to the achievement of purposes of social or economic development.

"The imaginary of society and power and the political imaginaries"

A naive conception of law tends to see it only as a system of norms designed to regulate social relations, ensuring those minimum standards of behavior for social coexistence to be possible. In this sense, the right would be limited to receiving social values, created by other spheres of cultural activity and giving them a binding force guaranteed by coercion.

In true, the creative (poetic) effectiveness of law is much greater. It not only creates peace and security. It also creates to a large extent the very values on which this peace and security are established. In this sense, law constitutes a cultural and social activity as creative as art, ideology or the organization of economic production.

In fact, before organizing it, law imagines society. Creates mental models of man and things, of social bonds, of political and juridical relations and then, latinically, gives an institutional body to this imaginary, also creating, for this, the appropriate conceptual tools. Entities such as "people" and "things", "men" and "women", "contract", "state", "sovereignty", etc., did not exist before jurists conceived them, conceptually defined and traced their dogmatic consequences. In this sense, law creates the very reality with which it operates. the "fact" does not exist before and independently of the "right". The "legal cases" really have very little to do with the "cases of life", as indeed becomes evident as soon as the doors of a court or the office of a lawyer are transposed.

"The history of law as a legitimating discourse"

Indeed, the history of law can play an opposite role to that which has been described, that is, it can contribute to legitimizing the established right.

Law itself is already a system of legitimacy, i.e. a system that fosters the obedience of those whose liberty will be limited by norms. In fact, law is part of a wide range of veiled mechanisms to build consensus on social discipline.

However, the law itself needs to be legitimized, that is, it needs to build a social consensus on the basis of its obligation, on the need to obey it. As we know from Max Weber (1864-1920), the legitimacy of political powers - that is, the answer to the question "Why is power legitimate?" - can be obtained from various belief complexes ("structures of legitimation"), organized around values such as tradition, charisma, rationalization (Weber, 1956) - that is,"because it is long established", "because it is inspired by God", "because it is rational or efficient". Within the legal world, some of these processes of legitimation - namely, "traditional" legitimacy - depend heavily on historical arguments.

Finally, relativism, if it is the basis of tolerance, is also the foundation of dialogue, since the acquisition of common positions, allowing the coexistence of differences can only be obtained by confrontation of opinions, compromise, open, programmatic and provisional consensus. (...)

Only a principle of response is advanced. Coexistence requires the existence of a minimum of common rules."

Marcus Tullius Cicero, talking about the stablishment of the Kings and the founding of the laws, said that in the end everything only lends itself to the conquest of glory and not to devotion to the republicae. He affirms that:

"The same cause was for the establishment of the laws; always being the end of these providences to obtain a justice equal to all, because otherwise it would not be justice. When they found this in a man of good and just, they were satisfied with him; but as not always could be obtained, they invented the laws."

In this work we start from the ethical and moral truth and not from legal truth, which we consider volatile, fluctuating and seasonal. Thus, every law cited must be interpreted as a metaphor and not as the paradigm of ethical truth with which public officials of Mercosur and all world public administrations should behave.

Sir Winston Churchill (1995.7: 13) in his memoirs suggests that positive law is not in itself capable of preventing disaster. Here is a precious excerpt from this thought:

"Winners and losers, to the same extent, still preserved the appearance of civilized states. A solemn peace was signed which, except for financial aspects impossible to enforce, conformed to the principles which had governed in the nineteenth century had relations among enlightened peoples. the rule of law was proclaimed and a worldwide instrument was created to protect us all, and especially Europe, from the resurgence of a convulsion."

The right of the last two centuries has crystallized into a positive-normative truth and has become one of the greatest debtor of morality and justice.

There has never been in time and legal space a moment in which we could say as we can since the beginning of the nineteenth century, *nom omne quod licet honestum est* (not everything that is legal is honest), a fact that did not escape the intellect of Eduard Moron Alcain (1998: 48) in analyzing the relationship between positivism and Nazism:

"Nuremberg" was interpreted as the adage *nullum crime sine lege* in a non-positivist sense (and that) the conviction that it was impossible to ignore these horrible crimes but which escaped a system of positive law has prevailed over the positivist conception of the foundation of the right ".

The old thesis that the creature follows its creator or that it has absolute relation with him is too relative to support itself. Many are the creatures who have become more prominent than their creators, like Quixote in regard to Cervantes, Sherlock Holmes in relation to Sir Arthur Conan Doyle, the state in relation to the man who created it.

Perhaps because of this, there are those who claim that in the right remains only remnants of morality. There are others like Radbruch, who firmly believe that law and morality are absolutely independent instances, as quoted by Neumann's in the following analysis:

Law and morals are each independent reference systems. In law, the point of reference of truth and correct pretensions is only the valid system of legal norms, so long as the legal program of decisions does not explicitly take into account moral standards. This means, in a negative way: The points of reference in any case are not unmediated pretensions of justice and the objectively correct."

1.1 - Characteristics of legal rules

The law is composed of norms, principles and decisions. Among the various characteristics of the norms it is to be inferred whether it prescribes:

1– an obligation;
2– an authorization; or
3– a prohibition.

Von Wright Apud Inmério Jorge Catenacci explicit:

"It is an obligation when something must be done; it is an authorization when something can be done, and it is a prohibition when something does not have to be done."

Therefore, the content of the standard is directly related to:

1) what should be done;
2) what can be done; and
3) What not to do.

It does not seem reasonable to accept that deontology has its origin in the norm, because it only crystallizes the will, the human feeling that, in turn, thirsts in the reasoning.

What to do or what should not be done in society is ethical and moral reflection that finds in law its form or formula of positive expression.

The modern States seems to have found in Law, the perfect formula for manipulating ethics and morality, since through the objective norm the truth that most interests the dominant ideology, can be crystallized.

The Law with its positive truth came to rule over peoples in such a way that the Brazilian Constitution, in its article 5 says that no one shall be obliged to do or not to do otherwise than by virtue of law.

The redeeming positivism in these messianic objective norms has shown a merely formal efficacy, as analyzed by Eduardo Morón alcain (1998: 69, 72):

"toda norma jurídica sea ella justa o injusta, pretende establecer o establece un deber jurídico. (...) uno puede perfectamente decir que en la Alemania nazi la SS tenía el deber jurídico de aprehender a los judíos y enviarlos a los campos de concentración (...) Pero en el sentido real y absoluto de lo que de humano tiene el término deber', como apelación a una conciencia libre, tal deber, así sólo se llame "jurídico" y no moral. (..) "Los individuos deben comportarse como la norma lo estipula" (...) en todos estos casos se siente, se cree que el derecho debe ser obedecido (...) La Alemania nazi, el pueblo en general, los miembros de las SS, los jueces y juristas en general, tenían la convicción (...) ese derecho que ordenaba prisiones, torturas y muertes era y debía ser cumplido."

This is why we need to rethink Law, in order to make it return to be the architect of a just society, instead of being a mere political tool of personal wills of some elected groups to safeguard the interest of other groups.

The law only has efficacy if it is at the service of the common good. Otherwise, it is nothing more than abstract rule made to justify moments of domination.

1.2 - Logical structure of the moral norm and legal norm

It is common ground that a law is constituted by a general prescribing of conduct, whether for the obligation, authorization or establishment of the prohibition it imposes to people.

An omission directed to a conscious, free and determined purpose.

The result on which depends the existence of any criminal act typified in law, it is only attributable to the person who gave it cause.

We consider as a cause all action or omission without which the result would not have occurred. This is how the theory of finalism understands and how our Brazilian system works, for example.

1.2.1 - Logical structure of the moral norm

One of the oldest and unsurpassed conceptualizations of a person is that he is a thinking being, as Aristotle taught so well.

Thus, all the works of being must be analyzed in the light of the theory of cognoscente, which assures us that every norm, be it moral or juridical, has a logical-rational structure.

In our sense the moral norm can be structured as follows:

REASON> WILL> ACTION OR OMISSION> MORAL CONSEQUENCE.

Decomposing the equation we have:

1– reason as the foundation of every science. Who does not have the faculty of reasoning or will be represented or will be assisted, which implies that he does not have the legal capacity to self-determine;
2– conscious and free will, as a corollary of reason;
3– action or omission (corollaries of conduct) conscious and free driven by the will; and
4– the moral consequence that is individual and proceeds in the tribunal of conscience. The moral consequence is still timid in demanding external reprimand, despite the accession of new jurists to the understanding of norms-principles or principles-norm.

On the moral consequence we feel obliged to say that the new juridical orientation that is ruling over the legal principles, transformed the principle of morality in one of the foundations of the relation between Brazilian Public Administration, the public servant and the citizenship.

However, norms-principles or principles-norms does not cover the typology of conduct. In other words, judges still not accept to condemn an illegal action or omission based upon directly on norms-principles or principles-norms.

For Brazilian sytem of law, the principle of morality to produce an effective sanction, still needs an action or omission, positively written that matches perfectly with what is written in a penal law, for example.

The illegal conduct is studied over through his objective and subjective elements, principal and accessory commands. If the confluence of all this factos matches to what is written in the positive prohibition of the law, so, the sanction may be applied.

For instance, the multiplicity of codes of Ethics in the Mercosuline Public Administrations, where the envisaged sanction is a mere moral censorship.

1.2.2 - Logical structure of the legal norm

The structure of the legal norm is different because the reason moves in the direction of law, passing almost always by the filter of morality, and then flows into a commissive or omissive conduct that generates a legal consequence. Here is a possible framework for the rule of law:

REASON > MORAL > RIGHT > ACTION OR OMISSION > LEGAL CONSEQUENCE.

Decomposing the legal equation we have:

1– Reason as the foundation of every science. Who does not have the faculty of reasoning or will be represented or will be assisted, which implies that he does not have the legal capacity to self-determine;

2– The Moral in some cases is the "filter" of the right. It is built with residue of that, because if the reason ingives the ability to discern what knowledge presents to us as "truth", whether scientific or not, norms, principles and decisions, in theory, will be filtered by the imposed or acquired moral;

3– The law is broken down into norms, principles and decisions, according to Imerio Jorge Catenacci (2006: 31) for whom Kaufmann rightly argues that no legal decision can be obtained solely from the legal norm.

We adhere to the conception of norms-principles or principles-norms, which are interrelated to regulate conduct.

4– Action or omission are the corollaries of threatening or harmful conduct. To the Law, the conduct will only be relevant when the action or omission that compose it is practiced conscious and free;

5– The legal consequence for cases of non-compliance with the standard may vary from a deconstruction of the right granted or delegated to a threat of punishment or sanction. The application of sanction without due process of law, in turn, invalidates legal acts from the origin (ex tunc effect).

It is important to remember that sanction is not an element of validity of the norm or principle, but condition of its efficacy. Without the sanction the prescriptive norm of an obligation, hypothetical authorization or prohibition, rarely fulfills its desiderato in time and space, although its end be the justice, as well said Catenacci (2006: 159):

"La finalidad del derecho. – Oportunamente caracterizamos el derecho como el ordenamiento social coercible de las acciones humanas según un criterio de justicia. De este concepto surge que el derecho tiene una finalidad: el orden social justo. El elemento justicia es esencial al derecho, ya que no podríamos llamar derecho a un orden predominantemente injusto."

1.3 - Categorical norms and hypothetical norms Categorical is the norm whose application derives from its own content. There are no conditions imposed for the implementation of the will of the legislator.

Hypothetical is the norm that requires other conditions not inferred from its content to produce the result determined by it, examples of which are the norms of international law that depend on the approval of national legal orders to give efficacy to their treaties and conventions.

The norms together with the principles and the decisions make up a juridical system, under the integrative perspective of the hermeneutic activity.

So the Constitution as a major rule must contain all the others and all the others must be contained in it, forming the national legal order.

Since the dawn of its existence, the world has been moving towards military, commercial, industrial and technological globalization, which is why the conflict and the law are inseparable.

Juridical-political globalization is also an old reality, as prove the alliances between city-states in antiquity (the Peloponnesian alliance, The Pact of Delos, etc.), and reached our time with alliances to which we nominate of economic blocs, such as European Union (EU), NAFTA - The North American Free Trade Agreement, Mercosur, etc.

The solidity of such integrations derives directly from hypothetical norms such as treaties and conventions whose contents are norms, principles and legal decisions of international law, gradually absorbed by national rights.

The lesson of Miguel Reale in Philosophical and Law Studies (1978: 81) is revealing when he says that all juridical interpretation necessarily takes place in a context, that is to say, in function of the overall structure of the organization (the integrated nature of the act interpretative).

The Professor Inocêncio Mártires Coelho, in Advanced Course of Brazilian Constitutional Law says that the understanding of the legal order is given by means of three rules of interpretation. Behold in his words (2003: 234-235):

" (...) from the postulate that the legal order is omni-comprehensive (in other words, encompasses everything), operational and coherent, three rules of interpretation are extracted:

a) The provisions of the Constitution reach all social relations, either by expressly regulating them or by assuring to the citizen who ask for jurisdiction to a court to rule on a conflict, those free spaces of the right which all need for the full development of the personality,

b) There are no rules left over in the Constitutional text. All are in force and operative, and it is incumbent on the interpreter to only discover the scope of incidence of each one, instead of admitting that the constituent, rational also from the economic point of view, may have spent more than one word to say the same thing: and,

c) There are no real conflicts between the rules of the Constitution, only apparent conflicts, either because they came into force jointly, either because there is no hierarchy or order of precedence between its provisions."

1.4 - Validity of the legal system

All legal norms form both national and international legal orders. How to give credit or lend validity to the legal order or to the coercive power of the law if the state does not fulfill its obligations in the social contract, by which the people give it legitimacy to represent it?

The people are destined to obey a power that legitimizes itself as part of the Social Contract of Rousseau, that guarantees citizenship and dignity, that exists to less than 20% of the world population. In this situation will not citizens be authorized or legitimated to exercise the right of resistance, against governments that disregard their obligations in the Social Contract?

David Baigun and Nicolás García Rivas say that right is the translation of the existence and operability of political power in a state of law and that politics has always pointed out as its nodal point the duty to obey the laws that legitimize it.

This is a stinging lesson of the authors cited:

"Sin duda la política es el marco natural y proprio donde se despliega el problema de la legitimidad, atada desde siempre a la legitimidad del poder político. Pero aquí ya no puede ser reducido a un problema interno a una rama del orden jurídico, sino que involucra a este en general, en su totalidad, porque el derecho es la traducción de la existencia y de la operatividad del poder político en un estado de derecho. (…)

La determinación del marco natural, de esa dimensión originaria, en la que se despliega el discurso de la criminología tiene otras consecuencias: la definición del crimen se desenvuelve en el terreno que la política, desde siempre, señaló como el tema central de la obligación política, esto es, el deber de obedecer las leyes, correlativo al poder de hacerlas cumplir y de aplicar las penas.

Corresponde a una de las caras del poder de imperium que desde la edad Media, comprendía el derecho del príncipe de pe- dir la riqueza o la vida de sus súbditos a través de los impuestos o de la llamada a las armas, y el de constituirse en juez para resolver las diferencias, aplicando la ley e imponiendo las penas.

Sólo así, en la perspectiva de un deber de obediencia sustentado en el reconocimiento de la validez del orden normativo y del poder coactivo que la ley implica, se comprende la importancia que para la concepción del estado tenía la pretensión de monopolizar el ejercicio de la fuerza, fuerza que, desde siempre, debe tener como atributo la legitimidad."

David Baigun and Nicolás García Rivas also deal with the legitimacy of the legal system and its crisis, emphasizing the impossibility of conceiving of a normal and just right when levels of inequality and structural violence are high or impede development. That is how they approach the question (2006: 96-97, 99-100):

"En concreto, esta idea de la sociedad requiere atender dos órdenes de problemas. El primero es el relativo al contenido de los fines comunes, que no son otra cosa que el conjunto articulado y sistemático de los intereses individuales, contenidos en un tramado básico formado por las condiciones mínimas de salud, seguridad, educación y justicia que comunidad y el estado consideran indispensables para su funcionamiento. El restante consiste en las formas que debe adoptar la convivencia a lo largo de dicho proceso. El sistema de las libertades, derechos, limitaciones y procedimientos que instituye la ley constituye el tejido formal de la convivencia. Se establece allí lo prohibido, las sanciones y los procedimientos. (...)

La degradación del derecho

Aunque en una perspectiva dirigida a desarrollar un control externo sistema penal, Alessandro Baratta ha precisado el problema de esta exacta manera:

"La normalidad del sistema penal es una consecuencia de la validez ideal y del respeto efectivo del pacto social, y por lo tanto de la vigencia de la constitución. Del pacto social la paz es por lo demás condición necesaria, pero no suficiente: las otras condiciones necesarias se deben buscar en la eficacia de las normas que regulan la organización y la división de los poderes del estado y garantizan los derechos fundamentales de los ciudadanos/hombres ... La utopía concreta de la alianza de las víctimas de la modernidad y de una reformulación del pacto social que garantice la 'inclusión de los excluidos' indica el recorrido para un proceso político de dimensiones planetarias que conduce, más allá de los límites del pacto social moderno, a formas más altas de 'desarrollo humano' en las cuales a relación entre necesidades, capacidades y derechos fundamentales alcanzará un nivel superior. Este camino de las luchas políticas pacíficas pasa también por una interpretación y una aplicación dinámica de la constitución de los estados sociales de derecho, por una política de desarrollo social y de protección integral de los derechos (derechos civiles, sociales, económicos, culturales y de participación política), protección que no es solamente la finalidad (indicada por lo menos bajo la forma de los principios generales de la acción estatal), sino también la garantía de funcionamiento de estas constituciones. Si no se recorre este camino, si el recorrido es obstaculizado o interrumpido, el desarrollo humano impedido, si se eleva el nivel de la desigualdad y de la violencia estructural en la sociedad, entonces no están las condiciones suficientes para la existencia de un derecho penal normal, aunque se haya realizado en todo o en parte la condición necesaria: la paz".

Baratta señala aquí la imposibilidad de concebir un derecho penal normal cuando el nivel de la desigualdad y de la violen- cia estructural se elevan o se impide el desarrollo humano. El contenido excede a las palabras. No se refiere meramente a la desigualdad o a las violencias sociales, que forman parte de las experiencias que acompañan la condición humana, contra las que la acción de los hombres reacciona bajo la forma de la política y del derecho."

On the other hand, Julio E. S. Virgolini, when dealing with topics such as politics and criminology, law and violence, says that the presence of the law must represent the eviction of violence because they are antagonistic fields that can not live together.

From the perspective of the legal-political relationship that democratic states of law have adopted, where there is no law there is violence. Now, if law is the form of social expression by which man claims his freedom and social equality, then he is the only protection against the arbitrariness of that same state of law.

Here is how Virgolin (2004: 265,267) punctuates such thing:

"De esta manera, el derecho, que es la forma de expresión típica del poder político, se convierte en el medio y en la garantía específicas de la identidad de ciudadano, sin las cuales éste no puede percibirse ni expresarse como tal. Y ello deriva de una doble relación de pertenencia, del ciudadano a la nación y de la nación al ciudadano, en igualdad con los otros hombres, que sólo puede ser expresada en el lenguaje del derecho. Sin la presencia del derecho, esa relación sólo puede ser violenta.

Porque el derecho es el único medio que a la vez sirve para reconocer, para establecer y para delimitar la libertad y la pro- piedad, esto es para instituirlas como las condiciones esenciales de la convivencia entre los hombres. Estas condiciones requieren tanto de bases materiales como de una protección jurídica: se trata, en este caso, de la necesaria protección contra la arbitrariedad del poder y contra el abuso de los otros hombres; en palabras más definitivas, de una protección contra la violencia. (...)

La relación que se establece es inversa: la presencia de la ley es la condición para el desalojo de la violencia; la ausencia de la ley llama en causa a la violencia. Las condiciones a las que se sujeta el ejercicio de la violencia legal corresponden a un nivel distinto, simplemente operativo, que se refiere a la racionalidad instrumental del sistema, a su justificación como instrumento adecuado para la persecución de un fin cuya legitimidad se halla en otra parte, que es el ámbito donde ha sido determinado.

De esta manera, el ciudadano es un sujeto que existe y actúa en un espacio instituido por el derecho, y que sólo a través de la lógica interna al derecho puede reclamar que ese espacio esté exento de violencia."

On the task of expressing norms of coexistence and of good government few lessons are as lapidaries as that of professor Manuel Hespanha (2005: 94-97):

"Consensual, ie obtained from the multiplicity of personal views, understood as views of the common good, but followed by a "substantive" political discussion, which confronts these perspectives and evaluates them in a dialogical way.

On the other hand, they must be minimally substantial (almost wholly procedural), in order to allow different values to coexist. On the other hand, they should be considered as provisional, susceptible of revision and, if necessary, not monotonous in their application, that is, variables according to a careful interpretation of each situation.

Given these principles, lawyers have two important roles to play.

On the one hand, lawyers, as specialists, have to guarantee the validity of these principles which we will call constitutional - against their daily deterioration.

Without prejudice to the fact that these principles are mutable and open, they constitute a very important nucleus of rules of coexistence, whose establishment (positivation, constitutionalization) was based on a series of cautions, designed precisely to ensure that they express common sense of the "republic". To ensure its change is possible, but must follow equally careful processes. It can not, on the other hand, be based on judgments of the temporary opportunity of a majority in power; nor of inorganic, little tried and emotional movements of public opinion. The jurists are responsible for this vigilance so that the structural and permanent one does not use to the taste of the conjectural of momentary. This involves, in turn, two tasks. The first is to identify, among emerging values, which correspond to, either (i) the mere claims of a part of society (of a group against the all, of the other groups ("whole") against a group; or (ii) to ephemeral values (for example, the exacerbated desire for security that accompanies a state of social insecurity); or (iii) the opportunistic values of those who govern (v.g., the need for reform must justify the omission of constitutional forms; the guarantors of legality are "blocking forces", to use a phrase recently in vogue).

This task of fixing norms of coexistence and good governance is even more important in today's world, where globalization (in spatial terms) and superabundance and frenzied succession of the senses (in temporal terms) created, from the difference of values, an indifference to values. At the same time, in field of social normativity the illusion of free choice has made seduction and temptation tend to substitute for the norm (Pierre Bourdieu). As Z. Bauman observes - glossing the "withdrawal of God" from the explanation of the world order, operated by normalists and humanists (see below, "dissolution of corporatism and

19

the advent of the individualist paradigm.") it is as if society no longer counts on social regulation (etiamoi sociat non esse), all giving rise to an anarchic, fleeting, superabundant and unrewarding profusion of values (Bauman, 2001,130 ss.).

It is then up to lawyers to re-rooted people in common values and thus to rebuild social order (and a sense of community and security).

The special legitimacy of jurists to carry out this diagnosis stems from their technical specialization; but above all (or exclusively) if it focuses on the "right in society", since only the consideration of the legal technique and the knowledge of society can lead to a correct evaluation of the values to be elected as constitutional values. The reference to "law in society" also involves the awareness of the very recognition of the social insertion of the jurists themselves of the politically determined nature (at various levels) of their discourse. On the other hand, the lawyers should try to establish routines to apply these principles.

That is, to test sequences of processes and reasoning (regulae artis) that give greater probability to the good application of these legal principles. Distinguishing situations, interpreting cases, testing the application of rules, formulating concept that synthesize acquired results. Always bearing in mind the idea that all these processes and concepts are provisional, not having a guaranteed success in the nth case (the future dog, not tried)."

1.5 – The right to resist any unjust rule of positive law

In the current context of our civilization there seems to be no doubt that the state is the greatest formula of expression of Political Power and that the constitution as its Fundamental Statute creates a dichotomy between constitutional state of law and judicial state of law in the search for nation and implementation of the "fair".

Law follows its path as a kind of technique or tool of social organization, dictating the rights, obligations and rights of those who live in society, while morality and ethics are shifting because they change over time, everything wears out, which is why constitutions can be modified by a constituent power, by a qualified majority or by a revolution, when the will of the people imposes itself.

Ferrajoli, quoted by Manuel Hespanha, is right when says that the content of a constitution will depend on the political-juridical will of the moment. Hespanha still says (2005: 95-96):

"En mi opinión, el constitucionalismo de Ferrajoli, aunque sin pretenderlo, se mueve de forma ambivalente entre estas dos formas de constitucionalismo. Por una parte, cuando Ferrajoli insiste en la compatibilidad con el positivismo, es muy claro afirmando que una constitución es una norma positiva, «puesta», que podría no haber existido y que podría tener un contenido totalmente diferente. Para Ferrajoli la constitución forma parte del derecho por su origen y los principios constitucionales solo son aquellos que fueron «puestos» en su momento. Al mismo tiempo, este autor también indica que los textos constitucionales reflejan y positivizan «aquellos derechos elaborados por la tradición jusnaturalistas que están en el origen del estado moderno, como "innatos" o "naturales"».
Por otra parte, Ferrajoli considera que la constitución tiene una doble naturaleza contractual: se fundamenta en un pacto hipotético que positivizaría ciertos derechos naturales y, a la vez, constituye un pacto histórico fruto de las luchas sociales y la negociación política. Por último, a pesar de que Ferrajoli asume que el contenido de una constitución dependerá de la voluntad político-jurídica del momento (DyG 105-107), también asume que está en la propia lógica del constitucionalismo la exigencia de que las constituciónes se expanden en tres sentidos: protección de derechos sociales, limitación de los poderes privados y alcance mundial. Me detendré un momento en este último punto. (CARBONELL, Miguel; SALAZAR, Pedro (eds.). Garantismo: estudios sobre el pensamiento jurídico de Luigi Ferrajoli. Madrid: trota, 2005. (colección estructuras y procesos serie derecho). p. 95-96.)"

David Baigun and Nicolás Garcia Rivas (2006: 102-103) sustain the right to resist against unjust governments, in the following words:

> *"Se trata de la raíz política del problema del crimen y el castigo, para la cual, en este umbral último, reaparecen dos términos ilustres de la ciencia política: la tiranía y el derecho de resistencia; han sido olvidados, y casi no aparecen en el vocabulario de las preocupaciones habituales o en la literatura reciente, y jamás en los textos de la criminología, y ello a causa no sólo de la disolución de lo político, sino principalmente de esa apariencia de estación terminal que ha asumido la sociedad occidental de capitalismo avanzado, bajo el espejismo de la lejanía de los horrores del nazismo. (...)*
>
> *Y estas realidades no soportan sólo una descripción material. Representan en cambio la más grave crisis del estado de derecho y del principio representativo y por ello, para utilizar el lenguaje de la política clásica, debería repensarse el uso del término tiranía como la expresión adecuada a la privación del derecho y de la cosa común que se manifiestan y difunden a través de la corrupción y de la exclusión social."*

The Law conforms to the political will of the moment. Thus, there is no reason to deny the right of resistance of the people whenever the government disobeys its part in the social contract, as provided in art. 1 of the Virginia Declaration of 1776. Here is the quote:

> "III-That government is instituted, or should be instituted, for the common purpose, protection and security of the people, nation, or community; that of all forms and forms of government this is the best, the most capable of producing greater happiness and security, and the one that is more and more securely insured against the danger of bad government; and that if a government proves to be inadequate or contrary to such principles, the majority of the community has the undisputed, inalienable, and irrevocable right to reform, alter

or abolish it in a manner deemed more in keeping with the
public good. (our underlining)

Aware that Law and Justice are distinct battlefields and above all that
Justice always wants Law and that Justice does not always want justice, I
am convinced that the Right of Resistance written in The Declaration of
the People of Virginia (1776) should be considered as the inalienable right
of the citizen.

We must consider that the state was constituted to promote the common
good and if it is used by governments that only care about their own
interests, these governments have to be deposed by the people.

CHAPTER 2

Anti-Corruption Criminal Law in Mercosur.

There is in the national legal systems of Mercosur, criminal legislation to combat crimes, as well as administrative and disciplinary norms against acts of administrative improbity. What is lacking is the application of such standards.

By way of example, we mention the legislation of the members of the Mercosur, only an article of their own codes, as a way of demonstrating what we have just said.

Argentine Penal Code:

"ARTICULO 261. – Será reprimido con reclusión o prisión de dos a diez años e inhabilitación absoluta perpetua, el funcionario público que sustrajere caudales o efectos cuya administración, percepción o custodia le haya sido confiada por razón de su cargo. Será reprimido con la misma pena el funcionario que empleare en provecho propio o de un tercero, trabajos o servicios pagados por una administración pública."

Brazilian Penal Code:

"Peculato

Art. 312 - appropriate the public official of money value or any other movable asset, public or private, of which he has the possession by reason of the position, or to divert it, for his own or other people's benefit:

Penalty - confinement, from two to twelve years, and fine.

Paragraph 1 - The same penalty applies if the public official, while not possessing the money, value or property, subtracts it, or competes for it to be subtracted, for his own or others' benefit, by availing himself of a facility which provides him with the status of public servant.

Paraguayan Penal Code:

"Artículo 300.- Cohecho pasivo

1º El funcionario que solicitara, se dejara prometer o aceptara un beneficio a cambio de una contraprestación proveniente de una conducta propia del servicio que haya realizado o que realizará en el futuro, será castigado con pena privativa de libertad de hasta tres años o con multa."

"Uruguayan Penal Code:

"Artículo 153. (Peculado)

El funcionario público que se apropiare el dinero o las cosas muebles, de que estuviere en posesión por razón de su cargo, pertenecientes al Estado, o a los particulares, en beneficio propio o ajeno, será castigado con un año de prisión a seis de penitenciaría y con inhabilitación especial de dos a seis años."

"Venezuelan Penal Code:

"Artículo 199º

Todo funcionario público que por retardar u omitir algún acto de sus funciones o por efectuar alguno que sea contrario al deber mismo que ellas imponen, reciba, o se haga prometer, dinero u otra utilidad, bien por si, bien por medio de otra persona, será castigado con presidio de tres a cinco años. El presidio será de cuatro a ocho años si el acto cometido ha tenido por efecto:

1) Conferir empleos públicos, subsidios, pensiones u honores, o hacer que se convenga en contratos en que este interesada la administración a que pertenece el funcionario

2) Favorecer o causar algún perjuicio o daño a alguna de las partes en un juicio civil, o al culpable en un proceso penal. Si del acto ha resultado una sentencia condenatoria restrictiva de la libertad individual, que exceda de seis meses, el presidio será de tres a diez años."

However, in relation to the scope of the fight against corruption with public goods, moneys and rents within Mercosur, which we intend to address in this work, the transcribed national legislation is conceived only with an internal perspective.

There are no criminal or administrative disciplinary norms that punish public servants and private citizens when they commit crimes or acts of extraterritorial improbity, in partnership.

Of the comparative analysis from the legislation of Mercosur, we find that the lack of effectiveness in the fight against corruption lies mainly in the following factors:

1– Dispersed criminal law;
2– Criminal procedure Legislation dispersed;
3– Scattered administrative legislation;
4– Scattered administrative disciplinary procedural law;
5– National judicial powers without jurisdiction to prosecute perpetrators of crimes and acts of improbity whose effects are freely and consciously planned to occur extraterritorially;
6– Lack of a specialized administrative court with competence to prosecute acts of impropriety against the Mercosur Public Administrations, when the effects extrapolate the frontier of the victimized country.

We studied the annals of the meetings of the Supreme Courts of Mercosur, just as we attended one of them in Brasília, Brazil, and realized how much discussion about constitutional asymmetry was an obstacle to the integration of the bloc.

In this work we intend to investigate corruption from different perspectives.

We believe, from the bibliography and other data collected, to have abundant legal material to prove the existence of constitutional and infra constitutional symmetry capable of allowing Mercosur to take a step beyond integration, ie, from the existing symmetry, unite criminal, administrative, and administrative disciplinary legislation to combat crimes and acts of misconduct against Mercosuline Public Administrations.

There is even doctrinal symmetry, since what Jorge Luis Rimondi says in Argentina about the crime of bribery is the same thing that is said synchronously and diachronically in any Mercosur country, that is, the semantics is the same. Let's read an excerpt from Rimondi (2000: 49-51):

"conforme con los antecedentes internacionales de interés para el tema, por cohecho debe entenderse a la acción de sobornar o corromper al juez o a cualquier otro funcionario público, a efectos de que, contra justicia o derecho, haga o deje de hacer lo que se le pide. Jesús Catalán Sender considera que su etimología se remonta al latín, derivándose al parecer de la voz confecere (en latín vulgar confectare y en castellano antiguo —siglo XIII— confeitar), equivalente a sobornar, corromper a un funcionario público. Como la mayoría de los delitos contra la administración pública, el cohecho encuentra su origen en el derecho romano. Siguiendo a Ferrini, puede armarse que tiene su primer antecedente legislativo en la Ley Calpurnia del año 149 a.C., a la que, en sentido similar, le siguieron la Junia, la Servilia, la Arcilia, la Cornelia y la Julia. En principio, contra estas conductas se le otorgaba a la víctima una acción de carácter privado, tendiente a lograr la repetición del monto respectivo por parte del autor, por lo que era conocida bajo el nombre de *crimen repetundarum*. A partir de la Ley Arcilia la acción civil se convirtió en penal, imponiéndosele al autor una multa del doble de lo recibido. Este sistema fue aplicado a varias figuras vinculadas con la corrupción en la administración pública, sin una clara distinción entre ellas. A modo de ejemplo, puede citarse la Ley Julia en la que por igual se sancionaba la aceptación de dinero para administrar justicia o cumplir un acto propio (actualmente denominadas "cohecho"), junto con la extorsión indebida de dinero (actualmente "confusión"). Conforme Garraud, es el código francés de 1792 el que caracteriza debidamente al cohecho, diferenciándolo del resto de las figuras con las que se mantenía confundido, a través de la motivación del autor. Así, el cohecho se configura cuando el funcionario público obra por lo que recibió o recibirá de acuerdo con lo convenido con el particular corruptor.

En la senda iniciada por la legislación francesa, doctrinariamente puede citarse a Carrara, quien definía a la corrupción (cohecho) como "la venta realizada entre un particular y un funcionario público, de un acto perteneciente al cargo de éste, que por regla debe ser gratuito (...)". (…)

En tal sentido, es dable citar la opinión de Jesús Catalán Sender, quien expuso: "Suele decirse en la doctrina italiana y española que si quisiéramos encontrar un nexo de unión a todas las diferentes tipologías de cohecho, un bien jurídico común, éste habría de ser necesariamente un bien jurídico común general, que bien podría ser el principio de imparcialidad (art. 103.3, infine, C.E.), o, lo que es lo mismo, que deben actuar neutralmente en todo momento, tiempo y lugar (principio de "eficacia indiferente" en conocida terminología del administrativista Garrido Falla)."

What is missing so that we have in Mercosur a penal, a procedural penal and administrative-disciplinary legislation unified against active or passive corruption? What is missing is a real political-juridical will, nothing more!

There is a transnational crime typology movement in Mercosur, but the criminal and administrative disciplinary treatment of the issue remains restricted to national legislation, rather than specializing in mercosuline justice that takes care of the application of persecutio criminis and jus puniendi of the state.

Rimondi also notes that in Argentina, until 1999, transnational bribery was not repressed. this is how it relates (2005: 119):

"Hasta el año 1999, nuestra legislación no reprimía al soborno transnacional. A fines de ese año entró en vigencia la Ley de Ética de la Función Pública, la que incorpora al código Penal dicha figura delictiva. Así, conforme al art. 36 de la norma citada, el art. 258 bis del cuerpo sustantivo reprimía al que "ofreciere u otorgare a un funcionario público de otro estado, directa o directamente, cualquier objeto de valor pecuniario u otro u otros beneficios como dádivas, favores, promesas o ventajas, a cambio de que dicho funcionario realice u omita realizar un acto en el ejercicio de sus funciones públicas, realizado con una transacción de naturaleza económica o comercial".

Do not think that what we said about the symmetry of crimes is restricted to the crime of bribery, nominated in Brazil as a bribe or active and passive corruption.

There are other hypotheses of symmetry in the typification of crimes against the Mercosur Public Administrations, such as:

1) traffic of influence;
2) embezzlement;
3) active corruption
4) passive corruption;
5) facilitation of smuggling or misplacement;
6) contraband;
7) misplaced;
8) white collar crimes;
9) extortion perpetrated by public servant;
10) prevarication.

If we take the analysis of Rimondi on the crime of extorsion perpetraded by public servant we will note full symmetry in the criminal understanding in force in Mercosur. This is what the author says (2005: 149-150):

> "Etimológicamente, el vocablo "concusión" proviene del latino concussio, que deriva a su vez de concutere que significa "sacudir". En consecuencia, con el término concussio se hace referencia a la acción de sacudir el árbol con el objeto de que caigan sus frutos. Este breve análisis etimológico permite la primera aproximación al delito, en el que la entrega de bienes no surge de la libre voluntad del dador, sino que es exigida por el receptor. Tal y como sucede con el nomen iuris, la figura en estudio encuentra su origen en el derecho romano. La concusión nace en roma—como la mayoría de los delitos contra la administración pública— dada la propia organización política de este pueblo de la Antigüedad, la que contrastaba con el abolutismo de los Estados contemporáneos, en los que

cualquier tipo de exacción reclamada por sus gobernantes era legal, por el solo hecho de que las exigencias partían de éstos. Ahora bien, los pasos iniciales de la concusión dentro del derecho latino no fueron sencillos.

Las primeras leyes que lo reprimieron eran aplicables a varias figuras vinculadas con la corrupción en la administración pública. A modo de ejemplo, puede citarse la Ley Julia, que bajo el término concusión no sólo incluyó la extorsión indebida de dinero (verdadera concusión), sino también la aceptación de dinero para administrar justicia o cumplir un acto del propio oficio (actualmente conductas atrapadas dentro del concepto de cohecho). La diferenciación del delito en estudio de la corrupción del funcionario público (cohecho) comienza realmente en la época imperial. Así, la concusión lentamente se va erigiendo como una forma independiente de extorsión. Sin embargo, la distinción llegó hasta tal punto que se utilizó el título de concusión para varios tipos de extorsión de disímiles caracteres. Por este exceso, autores posteriores (Carmignani, Carrara) debieron clasificar a la concusión como propia, cuando la extorsión era cometida por un funcionario público, y como impropia, cuando era ejecutada por un particular. De este modo, comenzó a tomar cuerpo la que es, aún en la actualidad, la formulación universal de este delito caracterizado por ser una extorsión cometida por un funcionario público, abusando de su autoridad para ello."

In the light of the foregoing, there is no doubt as to the existence of legal symmetry and, as this is the main prerequisite for the unification of criminal law, we believe that such an accomplishment can become efficient and promote the efficacy of the application of the jus persecuendi and the jus puniendi of the state, in the cases of crimes and acts of improbity that imply deviations from conduct related to acts of corruption with public moneys.

CHAPTER 3

Some Proofs of Simmetry among the Jurisprudence of Mercosur

The purpose of this work is not to analyze specific cases of corruption, but to demonstrate that there is legal symmetry capable of providing a link between criminal law, procedural law and administrative-disciplinary measures that deal with crimes and acts of improbity against Mercosur Public Administrations in the case of crimes with an extra-frontier scope.

We avoid casuistry because the acts of corruption, isolated or perpetraded in partnership are repeated in Mercosur more often than the beating of the wings of a hummingbird, whose frequency varies between 70 and 80 times per second. We know that sometimes it is a political strategy to practice one act to mitigate the other.

So we opted in this work for the scientific discussion that identifies the causes, the consequences, the allies and the guns to combat the phenomenon.

The importance of analyzing the jurisprudential aspect in the present case raises the symmetry of the legal system through the decisions of the national courts regarding the active subjects, against which there is a charge of corruption resulting from crimes against public administration and acts of administrative improbity that go beyond the borders of the country victimized by the illicit. Here are some examples that prove the symmetry of legal thinking (law, doctrine and jurisprudence) in countries of MERCOSUR:

3.1 - Argentina[1]

"REGISTRO DE CASOS DE CORRUPCIÓN Ficha N° 051

2007 (reaparición)
Caso Swift (Campell soup) Argentina casos vinculados - No
Resumen caso

La empresa de frigoríficos Estadounidense Swift, buscaba en el año 1990 radicarse en la argentina. En este proceso de radicación la empresa realizó una denuncia contra el Gobierno Nacional porque se le habrían pedido coimas para acelerar el proceso de asentamiento en la argentina. Esta denuncia fue respaldada por el gobierno de Estados Unidos quien, a través del entonces embajador, Terence Todman, quien envió una nota al Gobierno Nacional denunciando la situación.

La empresa quería importar maquinarias, que iban a ser utilizadas para ampliar su planta ubicada en la Provincia de Santa Fe sin pagar impuestos por US$4,4 millones, de acuerdo a la ley de promoción industrial. Se trataba de una inversión de US$140 millones. El pedido de coimas habría sido solicitado por Emir Yoma, cuñado y asesor del entonces presidente Carlos Menem, al frigorífico norteamericano Swift Armour. Como consecuencia de este caso, Emir Yoma debió renunciar a su cargo de asesor presidencial. Asimismo, el entonces Ministro de Economía, Antonio Erman Gonzalez, dejo su cargo a favor de Domingo Cavallo. Renunció además a su cargo el Ministro de Obras y Servicios Públicos, Roberto Dromi. La investigación judicial se encuentra cerrada sin que haya recaído condenas sobre funcionarios públicos.

Registro de casos de corrupción. disponível em: <http://www.transparenciacdh.uchile. cl/corrupcion/pdf/todos_los_casos.pdf>. acesso em: 11.05.2011.

3.2 - Brazil - (conviction for embezzlement) [2]

"PART: Paulo de Almeida Ivo e Souza and Superior Tribunal Militar
Abstract: Habeas Corpus. Criminal Proceedings. Patient condemned for
the crime of embezzlement in continuance of the offense. Allegation of
absence of Evidence for Recognition of Delinquent Continuity: Non-
occurrence. Absence of a defect in the statement of reasons. Precedents.
habeas corpus indeferido.
Rapporteur: Min. Carmen Lúcia
Judgment: 03/11/2008
Judging Body: First Class
Publication: DJe-070 DIVULG 17-04-2008 PUBLIC 18-04- 2008 EMENT
VOL-02315-04 PP-00944

Habeas Corpus. Criminal Proceedings. Patient condemned for the crime
of embezzlement in continuance of the offense. Allegation of absence
of Evidence for Recognition of Delinquent Continuity: Non-occurrence.
Absence of a defect in the statement of reasons. Precedents. habeas corpus
indeferido.

1– Constitutes a defect in the statement of reasons, and, therefore, this
   is a question exclusive of right, to examine whether the instances
   of merit provided evidence that could, even in theory, support
   the condemnation of the patient through two embezzlement
   procedures, in continuity of crimes. Precedents.

2– No need for exact description of the time and date of each of the
   subtractions in order to conclude that, since the goods subject to
   embezzlement in different were in different places and in different
   equipment, would not be a single action to be paid to the result.

3– habeas corpus dismissed."

Source: DJe-070 DIVULG 17-04-2008 PUBLIC 18-04- 2008 EMENT
VOL-02315-04 PP-00944.

3.3 - Paraguay [open case]

"REGISTRO DE CASOS DE CORRUPCIÓN Ficha N° 036

Año de aparición Nombre mediático del caso País en prensa 2005
Caso obra Pública Yacyretá argentina
Casos vinculados. No.
Resumen caso
En el año 1973, la argentina y Paraguay firmaron un tratado binacional que dio origen a la construcción de una represa hidro-eléctrica que lleva el nombre de Yacyretá. En el proyecto original, se previó una inversión de US$500 millones para conseguir su plena operación a mediados de los años 80. En 2008 dicho costo se había incrementado a un total de US$11 mil millones. Hay diversos hechos irregulares, entre otros pueden nombrarse: US$17 millones que se le pagaron indebidamente a la empresa italiana Ansaldo en concepto de reembolsos por cinco generadores que debían ser nacionales pero, en rigor, venían de Génova. En el 2002 Yacyretá renovó y dolarizó un contrato por US$42 millones con la consultora internacional Consorcio de Ingeniería de Yacyretá (CIDY) cuando "el trabajo lo podían hacer técnicos del estado", afirman expertos argentinos. Yacyretá, asimismo, renovó un seguro por la represa con la empresa británica Heath y según una auditoría implicaba un sobreprecio de US$1.500.000 por año. La represa se encuentra en funcionamiento actualmente. Sin embargo por las demoras en las obras no ha alcanzado su punto máximo de producción. Conducta/s reprochable/s estatus año de la conducta 39. Fraude: Malversación de fondos públicos/Peculado ilegal entre 1973 y 2008.

Actores implicados: Poder Ejecutivo de Argentina- Poder Ejecutivo de Paraguay - Empresa británica Heath - Empresa italiana ansaldo

3.4 - About Venezuela

In November of 2011, I stayed for a week conducting researches in Caracas, Venezuela. I have had almost unrestricted access to legislation in the Legislative Branch, but very difficult access to the datas of Judiciary

Branch and, given the political conditions in the country, we have chosen not to mention jurisprudence avoid misleading the veracity of the information.

We believe it is important to reiterate that the en of this work is not to prove the existence of corruption or the amount of money diverted from the public treasury of Mercosur member countries. First, because of the existence of corruption, we would expose ourselves to the truism by trying to prove something notorious. Second because governments do not disclose the truth about facts that they commit.

It is worth noting what was said by Carlos Gonzalez Puerto (2004: 5) in the Publication of the institute of studies in criminal and social sciences of Paraguay (INECIP), comparing the public official who fights corruption with Don Quixote and his windmills:

"Cuando un funcionario estatal, municipal o un ciudadano desafía a la corrupción, ya sea denunciando o persiguiendo casos concretos, en países como los nuestros que carecen de instituciones consolidadas, casi siempre cree que lo hace a manera de quijote contra molinos de viento, por la incomprensión que lo rodea y por la soledad en la que le suma su conducta. (...) Los mensajes que esta obra nos hace llegar son varios. La corrupción existe. Ella atenta sustancialmente contra la felicidad de los pueblos. Sus resultados son padecidos por todos nosotros, sabemos que la salud, la educación, la tierra, son bienes garantizados por la Constitución pero desatendidos por el Estado. No estamos solos. Una enorme cantidad de gobernantes, expertos, funcionarios y ciudadanos de todo el mundo piensan y trabajan para erradicar la corrupción. La sociedad civil de nuestro país se reúne de diversos modos, todavía inconexos, para denunciar y perseguir la corrupción. El futuro es de la ley. Sólo hay futuro en la ley, el futuro de los pueblos depende una hoja de ruta que los conduzca de un modo adecuado y certero. La hoja de ruta es la ley que impide que nuestra heterogeneidad termine por homogeneizar la arbitrariedad. La lucha contra la corrupción nos enaltece como seres humanos. A los gobiernos totalitarios los hemos sufrido todos los pueblos, la libertad se ha conseguido con luchas que

> han costado mucha sangre. La revolución americana, la revolución francesa no son cuentos rosas sino han sido luchas cruentas en pos de un futuro de libertad y felicidad.
> El estado corrupto debe ser vencido y la lucha franca contra sus manifestaciones nos engrandece."

Given its role in the interpretation of law, the decisions of the Courts of Justice almost as much as the law carries upon its people the popular hope in the fairness or just distribution of social dignity.

In Mercosur, we deem it important to register the creation of the Permanent Forum of Supreme Courts, whose meetings have served to rethink Mercosur law from the point of view of integration.

Here is an excerpt from one of the meetings whose theme was "Challenges and perspectives in the process of integration of Mercosul", in the year 2007 in Brasilia, Brazil:

"Created by the letter from Brasilia, the Permanent Forum of Supreme Courts of Mercosur is the result of the initiative of Presidents and representatives of Supreme Courts of Mercosur and associated Countries and Members to institutionalize the ongoing dialogue between the national Judiciary Branches on legal issues of relevance to Latin American integration.

The memory of the Permanent Forum of Supreme Courts of Mercosur registers several years of work and dedication by the region's judicial organs with a view to the approximation and cooperation between them, aiming at institutional evolution and strengthening of the integration process.

(...)

Reaping the experience of European Union and discuss the to establish a permanent jurisdiction for Mercosur, as well as the effectiveness of the block regulation, when applied by national Judiciaries branches.This permanent nucleus of interest was detailed and deepened year after year.

The second meeting dealt with the problem of constitutional asimmetries that impeded full integration, discussed the need for legislative harmonization in procedural and material law, and discussed the system of dispute settlement and the prospects of the newly installed Assumption Court.

The third meeting showed the need for diffusion of integrationist ideas so that the theme is no longer just an academic concern and of the ruling elites and is widespread among the population. To this end, representatives of the main press organizations and journalistic companies of the region were invited to the debate. At the same time, representatives of the large industry of the member countries approached, in a comparative manner, the persistent obstacles to the widest circulation of goods and capital within the bloc.

Finally, we wish to record that our proposal with this work is to provide elements so that Mercosur's political and juridical bodies, if they wish, can take a step beyond integration based on proven legal symmetry and thus bring about, as a means of fighting against corruption, the unification of material and procedural laws, as administrative-disciplinary legislation, creating a supranational justice that deal with crimes and acts of improbity against the Mercosur Public Administrations.

CHAPTER 4

Internal Legal Order of Combat of Corruption

The aim of the State-administration is to promote maximum collective well-being. This task goes through legal-political legitimacy, the public budget and, above all, by an efficient administration of human and material resources.

The modern states democratically legitimized by its Constitutional system, needs to strengthen its political-legal foundations to fight corruption in order to fulfill at least part of the promise of social development that originated its creation. Otherwise they won't reach stability. Nor economic nor social.

David Baigun (2006: 88-90) addresses the issue in the following way:

> "Y de esta forma, el verdadero problema de la corrupción es el de la corrupción política, esto es, el de la degradación del carácter público de los actos de gobierno que, por así decirlo, se han privatizado al haber sido adquiridos en base a unas reglas que han dejado de ser públicas, esto es, al alcance de todos los ciudadanos en las condiciones igualitarias prescritas por la ley, y que por eso se han degradado a simples bienes de mercado, cuyo acceso está determinado por la potencia individual o económica. (...)

> "De este modo el problema de la corrupción se incorpora a los tradicionales dominios de la ciencia política, en los que es central el problema de la naturaleza y del origen de las reglas que conforman el entramado de la convivencia

38

humana. En el amplio abanico de las cuestiones que ese problema abarca debe relevarse el desplazamiento del valor de la ley como meditación en la interacción social, que se ve degradado frente al predominio de reglas informales fundadas en relaciones personales o en lazos económicos. Y con ello el valor constitucional de la igualdad, entendido aquí como derecho a igual tratamiento en función de la igualdad de situaciones y como derecho de acceso a las prestaciones del estado con el solo título de la ciudadanía, se ve mermado o desconocido por el privilegio adquirido en condiciones de mercado.

(...)

La ley vale entonces para algunos lo que ha dejado de valer para otros, y ello implica, entre muchas otras cosas, un problema que desde el ángulo de las disciplinas que naturalmente suelen tratar la cuestión de la corrupción ha permanecido oscurecido: se trata del problema de la legitimidad."

The aim of public administrations is to provide maximum welfare for those who are managed, especially because the people have fulfilled their share of obligations in the Social Contract, while the state accumulates more and more social debt.

The question is: how can the Mercosur Public Administrations provide the maximum of social welfare?

We believe that the solution lies in making and realizing the social rights foreseen in constitutions and infra-constitutional laws. For this, it suffices that there is a political-juridical will.

It is no novelty to say that the art of governing belongs to the political sphere and to The Public Administration the management human and material resources of the state, in order to provide adequate public services. The first sphere make the planification and the second provides the execution for the development that provides the collective welfare.

Nor is it novelty to say that the public administration is allowed what the law allows and what the law does not mention does not authorize it to be done. This is so in Brazilian and Latin American administrative law.

The problem is that in spite of the notoriety of these truths, the public managers are in charge of governing and administering to the proper spirit, and not in the form of the law.

We present below the table with the comparative legislation of Mercosur member countries, as a way of continuing to demonstrate the existence of symmetry of the structure, and of Mercosur public administrations - MPAs.

Here are ten symmetries that stand out:

1– all administrations are headed by the President of the republic;

2– all are formed by a group of organs and public agents;

3– all are classified centrally and decentralized;

4– all are responsible for the provision of public services;

5– all are responsible for collecting and applying the public budget;

6– all have organic laws that govern them and are governed by the power bound, that is, their managers and employees are destined to act according to the law;

7– all are governed by the principles of legality and hierarchy, among others symmetrical;

8– all undergo internal control over budgetary, financial, asset and operational aspects;

9– all of them have external control over budgetary, financial, asset and operational aspects;

10–all the public administrations of Mercosur member countries use discretion to act in the field of Police Power and all have an administrative sanctioning right, as guardian of probity in dealing with the *res publicae*.

We present below an indicative framework of the organic laws of the Mercosur public administrations, knowing that they may undergo changes with time, as we have already said, our right is volatile, fluctuant and seasonal.

However, we are certain that the reading of the comparative tables that we elaborate will not lose its importance because we focus on ethics and morals, that is, on the science of the just However, we are certain that the reading of the comparative tables that we elaborate will not lose its importance because we focus on ethics and morals, that is, on the science of the just and this can't be changed by decree.

4.1 - Table - Organic Laws of the Mercosur Public Administrations

Argentina	Decreto N° 357/2002.- organigrama de aplicación de la Administración Nacional Centralizada hasta nivel de subsecretaría, objetivos de las unidades organizativas y ámbitos jurisdiccionales de organismos descentralizados. (...) Decreto N° 1283/2003.- Modifica la LEY DE MINISTERIOS en las competencias establecidas a través de los artículos 20 y 21(Ministerio de Economía y Producción y Ministerio de Planificación Federal Inversión Pública y Servicios
Brasil	Lei n. 13.502/2017 – dispõe sobre a organização da Presidência da República e seus Ministério (It changes constantely because in Brazil and Latin America, as in other fields, we don't have legal stability).
Paraguai	Decreto n° 630/24 de Octubre del 2008 Por la cual se establecen responsabilidades, funciones y competencias para la ejecución del proyecto denominado "Modernización de la Administración Pública en Paraguay", suscrito con la Comunidade Europea el 25 de Enero de 2006, aprobado por Ley n° 3158/2007.
Uruguai	Esta previsto na Constituição de 1967 que a estrutura do Poder executivo terá uma administração Pública organizada de forma centralizada e descentralizada, (artigos 149 e seguin-tes). - Ley n° 17.292/2001 (Publicada D.O. 29 ene/001 – n° 25695) – ADMINISTRACIÓN PÚBLICA Y EMPLEO, FOMENTO Y MEJORAS.

Venezuela	Ley Orgánica de la Administración Central Artículo 1: Este decreto Ley establece la estructura y rige el funcionamiento de la Administración Central, de sus órganos y sistemas, determina el número y denominación de los Ministerios sus competencias y las bases de su organización. (...) Artículo 3: La administración Pública sé organizará y actuará de conformidad con el principio de legalidad, por el cual la asignación, distribución y ejercido de sus competencias se sujeta al mandato de la Constitución de la República y las leyes.

Within Mercosur communities, people must have an unwavering will to unite around the common good, in order to force States to provide welfare for all, instead as only for some privileged classes.

Here is an excerpt from what Tocqueville said (1957.13: 103) about the concern of North American Governments with the welfare of their people, eventhough modern times shows this concern is vanishing:

> "No se encontrará nunca, por mucho que se intente, verdadero poder entre los hombres más que en el concurso libre de voluntades. Ahora bien, no hay en el mundo más que el patriotismo o la religión, que puedan hacer caminar durante largo tiempo hacia un mismo fin a la totalidad de los ciudadanos. (...)
>
> Lo que admiro más en Norteamérica, no son los efectos administrativos de la descentralización, son sus efectos políticos. En los Estados Unidos, la patria se siente en todas partes. Es venerada desde la aldea hasta la Unión entera. El habitante se liga a cada uno de los intereses de su país como a los suyos mismos. Se glorifica de la gloria de la nación; en los éxitos que ella obtiene, cree reconocer su propia obra, y se regocija por ellos. Se alegra también de la prosperidad general, de la que se beneficia. Tiene hacia su patria un sentimiento análogo al que se experimenta por

la familia, y es por una especie de egoísmo que se interesa por el Estado.

A menudo el europeo no ve en el funcionario público sino la fuerza; el norteamericano ve en él el derecho. Se puede decir, pues, que en Norte América el hombre no obedece jamás al hombre, sino a la justicia o a la ley."

The state has the duty to produce the following fruits for its citizens: work, health, education, housing, transport, security, leisure, among other social rights.

Luis Roberto Gomes (2003: 261) Public Prosecutor in São Paulo, aware of this truth has used the law as the frontier of this search. Here's how it addresses the issue:

> "Well. It was in the light of the instrumentality of the process that the public civil action, inspired by the American class action and instituted by Law n ° 7,347/85, emerged as an instrumental guarantee made available to society for the defense of these interests, which, although they existed, people had no way to plea by action to Judicial branch to defend them with the necessary effectiveness.
>
> According to Jose Carlos Barbosa Moreira, the remarkable development of the techniques of collective protection of supraindividual rights and interests in the last decades of the twentieth century, we owe to the influx of the US (Moreira, 2002. p. 126)
>
> On the other hand, the Brazilian legal system on the protection of diffuse interests, collective and individual homogeneous, has exerted influence in some Latin American legal systems, such as those of Argentina and Uruguay(Grinover. 2000, p.14)."

On the role of the judiciary in controlling the administrative omission that denies the basic rights of citizenship, Luis Roberto says with property:

"Luiza Cristina Fonseca Frischeisen recalled that, following the institutionalization of social rights, a process was followed for the reassignment of its guarantees, which led to a process of judicialization of these rights, since, among those guarantees, was the creation of mechanisms of judicial protection for its effective exercise (Frischeisen, 2000, p.97).

Such judicialization led to the phenomenon known as politicization of the Judiciary Branc, a role that goes beyond the solution of the individual conflict of private law inter part to incorporate a creative role of interpretation and content standards, such as art. 196 of the Magna Carta, for the realization of rights of the social order (Frischeisen, 2000, p.98).

But notice that it is not:

[...] of a Judge-in-Law or of the substitution of the Executive Branch by Judiciary Branch, but rather of a judge interpreting the Federal Constitution, who must be in tune with the demands of the different sectors of the society in which he lives (Frischeisen, 2000, p.103). (…)

As has been said by Urban Ruiz, the judge must be seen by the citizen as a guarantor of rights and:

[...] if modernly, the state must be seen as an implementer of public policies, in order to build a more just, equal and solidarity society, which the goal must be eradicate or minimize poverty (See article 3 of the Brazilian Constitution), it is possible to judicially demand that public administrators implement measures or policies that allow a more dignified and just life for each Brazilian citizen (Ruiz, 2001, pp. 254-255)."

One of the most important roles of the law is that of regent of society. In order to produce the desired effects, that is, to solve social conflicts and serve as a conduit for development, it needs to be fulfilled.

The political-juridical classes urgently need to understand that, it is not the amount of existing laws that promotes substantial democracy, but rather the implementation of public policies, because it is this demonstration of real respect for the public interest that makes the law and the state respected.

The rule between the application of the law and its credibility is absolutely proportional, that is, the more impunity, greater is the disbelief in law and in the State.

CHAPTER 5

Legislation on Ethics in Mercosur

Any honest discussion of ethics should consider the free and conscious will that leads us to do or to fail to do something.

Whoever knows that must do good and has the means to perform such a task and omits, failed with ethics, in other words, failed with the Justice.

Carlos Santiago Nino agrees with this thought when says:

"La idea de que una omisión es, salvo en casos especiales, menos mala desde el punto de vista moral que una acción positiva que tiene exactamente las mismas consecuencias nocivas parece gozar de una aceptación prácticamente universal. Pocas opiniones nos parecerían tan claramente exageradas como la afirmación de que, por ejemplo, un ministro de hacienda que no asigna fondos suficientes a los hospitales, con el resultado previsible de que cierto número de pacientes morirá por falta de atención médica adecuada, es tan moralmente reprensible como si pusiera una bomba en un hospital matando a igual número de pacientes. Como dice Philippa Foot, si bien consideramos que hay algo de malo en, por ejemplo, negarse a contribuir con donativos para comprar comida para algunos niños de la India que, de otro modo, morirán de hambre, todos estaríamos de acuerdo en que actuaríamos mucho peor si contribuyéramos con donativos para comprarles comida envenenada, aunque el número de víctimas fuera el mismo en los dos casos."

Rene Passet (2002: 221) talking about rights and duties says:

"According to Kant's categorical imperative, the rights and duties of one to another are based on one another: the right I have of you is the same as you have over me; Now, the future generations, which by definition have not yet been born, can not have, in relation to us, none of the duties that would serve as fundament for our duties, in relation to theirs."

Javier Gomá (2009: 263) in his excellent work "Ejemplaridad pública" afirmou que "La inmoralidad de los gobernantes difunde un ejemplo negativo que luego ellos mismos se ocupan de reprimir mediante leyes más severas y restrictivas de las liberdades". He still says (2009: 244):

"Las costumbres son imitaciones colectivas de una Ejemplaridad primaria, persuasiva, contagiosa, innovadora; en suma, carismática. Carisma es, en efecto palabra que designa la fuente de la influencia que la persona ejemplar ejerce en el círculo de su experiencia social.

Due the standards of justice\ to which he adheres, the man tends to live in crisis. this is because rational nature makes us ethical, valuing beings, as emphasized by Professor Rabinovich-Berkman:

"El humano es un valorador automático. No puede abstenerse de emitir juicios axiológicos. Puede no expresarlos, hasta reprimirlos dentro de su mente, pero no evitarlos. conocer algo, verlo, sentirlo, saber de su existencia, es valorarlo, sentir alguna reacción a su respecto. además, siempre percibe las cosas desde un punto de vista. No es omnisciente ni omnipresente, caracteres que se atribuyen a dios, en gran medida por contraposición al hombre."

It is through free will that we make choices. If for good or for evil it is a subjective decision, wholly arising from the will which we will treat here as a synonym of interest and always conceptualizing it as a conscious and free conduct directed to an specific end and this conduct is rationalized by our free will, as affirms the philosopher Arthur Schopenhauer (2006: 6):

> "...la doctrina de la determinación de la libertad humana, la cual sólo puede expresarse en el marco de ciertas restricciones, y el hecho mismo de desconocerlas o bien de eludirlas no impide en modo alguno que éstas actúen. Antes bien, su desconocimiento las involucra aún más; y es así que la pretendida libertad expresada en la fórmula: "Puedo hacer lo que quiera" se transforma en un "Puedo hacer lo que debo".
>
> El grado de libertad humana, si bien es mayor que el grado concedido a los animales, se ve restringido por la acción de ciertos determinismos estructurales que son insuperables por los actos de la voluntad. Entre ellos: la ley de la causalidad, el carácter, la condición humana y, finalmente, los motivos que condicionan y se imponen a la volición restringiéndola siempre en una dirección precisa."

The science of the just can not exist without its antithesis, and in this necessary dichotomy between "I can do what I want" and "I can do what I ought" is that ethics manifests itself, sometimes stratified in political, legal, medical ethics or administrative, but always with a unique sense of doing what is honest, just, moral. It is necessary to know that it is not the multiplicity of codes of ethics nor the grandiloquence of his commandments that makes man an ethical being.

We agree with Nicolás Garcia Rivas (2006: 132) when he refers to the "Codes of Ethics" as the "decalogues of the impossible".

Our emphasis on this work is about the ethical action of the public agents of any level or sphere of government, since they deal with the common good, with the collective interest, with the patrimony of the state, that is, with the patrimony of the people.

5.1 - Centrifugal corruption and centripetal corruption

Mariano Grondona was one of the pioneers to conceptualize the act and state of corruption and both seem to manifest from the inside out, that is, from the man to the state, since state as a political association is a late invention, compared to micro social groups such as family, tribe, clan, cities, etc.

In those small associations, centrifugal corruption is installed, which keeps moving away from the center to all other directions, as the group grows and accumulates wealth.

Centripetal corruption is a return to the center. occurs when the body grows large and power reaches the center of associations or institutions.

When man has united in this social superstructure, power has been so decentralized that its greater concentration has come to be located in the center, that is, in the functions of execution, legislation and jurisdiction of the state, which is why a post at its core, is so disputed.

Being a public body a bundle of attributions or a center of competencies formed by position, function and agent, each organ or entity of a public administration is a power center to demand of its managers the use of power in an ethical and moral way.

The abuse of power requires ethical, moral and juridical intervention, which is why the intervention of national and international law is necessary in order to reorient the conduct of the offender.

5.2 - The vision of International Law on Ethics

We will deal more fully with this in Book 4. However, it seems appropriate for us to say that the UN, which is aware of the destructive effect of corruption, has issued the UNCAC - United Nations Convention against Corruption, with a view to instigating signatory countries to incorporate into its national regulations, the ethical conduct of its civil servants.

Here it is an excerpt of de UNCAC quoted by the report of "Oficina Anticorrupción del Ministerio de Justicia y Derechos Humanos de Argentina" (2004: 30-31):

Article 8" Codes of Conduct for Public Officials, establishes that:

1. Con objeto de combatir la corrupción, cada Estado Parte, de conformidad con los principios fundamentales de su ordenamiento jurídico, promoverá, entre otras cosas, la integridad, la honestidad y la responsabilidad entre sus funcionaríos públicos.

2. En particular, cada estado Parte procurará aplicar, en sus propios ordenamientos institucionales y jurídicos, códigos o normas de conducta para el correcto, honorable y debido cumplimiento de las funciones públicas.

3. Con miras a aplicar las disposiciones del presente artículo, cada estado Parte, cuando proceda y de conformidad con los principios fundamentales de su ordenamiento jurídico, tomará nota de las iniciativas pertinentes de las organizaciones regionales, interregionales y multilaterales, tales como el Código Internacional de Conducta para los titulares de cargos públicos, que figura en el anexo de la resolución 53/59 de la Asamblea General de 12 de diciembre de 1996.

4. Cada estado Parte también considerará, de conformidad con los principios fundamentales de su derecho interno, la posibilidad de establecer medidas y sistemas para facilitar que los funcionarios públicos denuncien todo acto de corrupción a las autoridades competentes cuando tengan conocimiento de ellos en el ejercicio de sus funciones.

5. Cada estado Parte procurará, cuando proceda y de conformidad con los principios fundamentales de su derecho interno, estabelecer medidas y sistemas para exigir a los funcionarios públicos que hagan declaraciones a las autoridades competentes en relación, entre otras cosas, con sus actividades externas y con empleos, inversiones, activos y regalos o beneficios importantes que puedan dar lugar a un conflicto de intereses respecto de sus atribuciones como funcionarios públicos.

6. Cada Estado Parte considerará la posibilidad de adoptar, de conformidad con los principios fundamentales de su derecho

interno, medidas disciplinarias o de otra índole contra todo funcionario público que transgreda los códigos o normas establecidos de conformidad con el presente artículo."

Cincunegui (1996: 52, 56-57), addressing the Foreign Corrupt Practices Act north, which can be cited as the paradigm for the criminalization of corrupt practices that Brazil and Argentina inserted in their internal legal system, says:

"En 1977, bajo la presidencia de Jimmy Cárter, el gobierno de los estados unidos lanzó su ahora internacionalmente famosa Ley de Prácticas Corruptas en el Exterior.

A consecuencia de las averiguaciones del caso Watergate, los investigadores del congreso descubrieron inesperadamente, en 1974, que algunas compañías locales habían otorgado sobornos a partidos políticos y a funcionarios públicos de otros países. Una investigación posterior de la comisión controladora de acciones y valores (security and ex-change commission) reveló que más de trescientas empresas de los Estados Unidos habían incurrido en ese mismo tipo de prácticas. Desde el Congreso, el Departamento de Estado y otros organismos se sostuvo, entonces, la necesidad urgente de imponer penas a una conducta que fue considerada indigna desde el comienzo. Si bien la ley así surgida fue ampliamente divulgada y discutida en su país de origen desde su promulgación, sólo es popularmente conocida en el mundo ahora, cuando la corrupción pasó a ser un tema de debate internacional.

La Foreign Corrupt Practices Act (FCPA), cuya exégesis procuramos hacer en este capítulo, establece severas sanciones privativas de la libertad y pecuniarias para las empresas y ciudadanos particulares de los Estados Unidos que, con el fin de conseguir o conservar un negocio, otorgaren sobornos a funcionarios gubernamentales del exterior, partidos políticos, funcionarios o candidatos de partidos políticos del exterior.

A consecuencia de esa ley, las empresas de los Estados Unidos perdieron muchos contratos, a lo largo de veinte años, que probablemente fueron a parar a manos de empresas de otros países sobre las que no pesaban las graves sanciones con las que la FCPA amenaza a las compañías norteamericanas. Hasta la firma de la Convención Interamericana Contra la Corrupción, en marzo de 1996, ningún país había asumido un compromiso internacional semejante. Estados Unidos lanzó su campaña en favor de la ética sin contrapartida económica ni política. Sus empresas perdieron contratos y el gobierno dejó de recibir millonadas sumas en concepto de impuestos a las ganancias que hubieran generado los contratos perdidos. Pero un nuevo estilo había comenzado. (...)

VIII.I. Introducción al sistema norteamericano.

VIII.I.1. La Regulación de Standards de Conducta Ética.

Los empleados del Gobierno Federal de los EEUU deben "cumplir con los altos niveles de conducta ética" cuando sirven al público. Se considera que "cada empleado es responsable, frente al Gobierno de los estados unidos y sus ciudadanos, de ser leal a la constitución, a las leyes y a los principios éticos ...."

Las regulaciones sobre los niveles de conducta para los empleados del gobierno federal de los EE.UU. se encontraban contenidas en la Orden Ejecutiva N° 11.222, dictada por el presidente Lyndon B. Johnson en 1965. Pero como parte de un movimiento general para revisar y actualizar las mismas, George Bush ordenó en 1991 a la oficina de Ética del Gobierno (OGE) que en base a aquéllas, formulara un conjunto de normas singulares, comprensivas y claras. Esta última, una vez cumplimentados los requerimientos de la Ley de Procedimientos Administrativos, efectuó diversas modificaciones que incluyeron una gran variedad de cuestiones: permisibilidad a un empleado del gobierno, en su calidad de tal, de aceptar regalos por una fuente ajena al gobierno o por otro empleado gubernamental; conflicto de intereses financieros; imparcialidad en el ejercicio de funciones o facultades oficiales; búsqueda de empleo; abuso de posición; y actividades extraoficiales, las que fueron parcialmente aprobadas por la Regla Final N° 57 el 7 de agosto de 1992, actualmente vigente.(...)

VIII.L2. Otras normas vinculadas a la lucha contra la corrupción.

Breve referencia sobre la denomina acción "qui tam" y la Whistle Blower Act (WPA).

'Qui tam' es una abreviación de la frase latina 'qui tam pro domino rege quam pro si ipso in hac parte sequitur' que significa que 'Quien demanda en beneficio del rey lo hace también en beneficio propio' ('Who sues on behalf of the King as well as for himself').

Se trata de una acción iniciada por un informador en base a una norma legal que establece una penalidad por la comisión u omisión de determinado acto, pudiendo ser recuperada en una acción civil, correspondiendo parte de dicha penalidad al demandante. (...)

Un "whistle-blower", por su parte, es un empleado que se rehúsa a comprometerse en actividades ilegales de su empleador.

Las Whistle-blower Acts son las leyes federales o estatales que protegen a los empleados que denuncien las irregularidades o ilícitos cometidos por los empleadores. La Civil Service Reform Act (5 U.S.C.A. & 2302 (b)), por ejemplo, protege a los empleados federales que denuncien este tipo de actividades. Muchas otras leyes federales protegen a los empleados que denuncian irregularidades, por ejemplo, la O.S.H.A. (29 U.S.C.A. & 660 (c)).

Los denominados 'whistleblowing' son informes de empleados sobre hechos vinculados a comportamientos inmorales llevados a cabo por sus empleadores y/o empleados del gobierno, estimulados a través de leyes que protegen al 'whistleblower' (denunciante). Esta protección, sin embargo, si bien puede no alcanzar al despido, puede tener efectos sobre el mismo."

I would like to conclude this chapter by reproducing the "Model of conducts" quoted by Juan Bautista and Juan de Dios Cincunegui (1996: 74), in which in the first column describes the employee's acting corrupt, in the middle column the employee's relative ethics or neutral values and the last column describes the conduct of the ethical officer.

The "behavior models" framework was made available to the public by Corruption in land Use and Building Regulation. Vol. 3, An Anticorruption Strategy for Local Government (Menlo Park, California: SRI International, January, 1978).

His analysis leads us to a detailed understanding of the three most traditional practices of public agents. if you have the patience and interest to pursue academically, you will fully understand how the:

1— corrupt employee;
2— employee of relative ethics and neutral values;
3— ethical employee.

This is why, with the due credits to which it has elaborated, I reproduce it in its entirety:

"MODELS OF CONDUCT"

Funcionario Corrupto	Funcionario de Etica relativa o valores neutrales	Funcionario ético
No brinda incentivos para una comunicación veraz y abierta ni para la autoexpresión, lo cual conduce a la retención de la información o del consejo que puede resultar impopular o desfavorable.	Se concentra en hechos, razones, verdades con validez empírica, mientras tiende a divorciar todo interés por la honestidad y la sinceridad de propósitos sociales mayores.	Fomenta la comunicación veraz y abierta y la autoexpresión a través del ejemplo, de establecer un clima, y de otros modos ade-cuados.
No brinda incentivos para una buena tarea.	Basa el sistema de incentivos en una de definición muy estrecha de lo que significa una buena tarea.	Brinda incentivos para una buena tarea.
Restringe el desarrollo y las contribuciones de los demás.	Restringe e cazmente el desarrollo y las contribuciones de los demás.	Estimula el desarrollo y la contribución de los demás.
Se encarga de que aquellos que no prestan servicios en pos del interés público sean removidos del servicio si no modifcan sus métodos.	No está de acuerdo con un concepto público bueno del interés público y no ve ningún modo válido de establecer criterios basados en valores para determinar lo que eso no es de interés público.	Se encarga de que aquellos que no cumplen con el interés público sean removidos de la función pública si no cambian sus modalidades.
Utiliza el poder de modo autoritario, coercitivo o maquiavélico.	Considera el poder en términos de equidad, uniformando las relaciones de poder, interesándose más por la imparcialidad del proceso que por el propósito humano y social alcanzado por el proceso.	Considera al poder como una fuerza creativa que se autogenera para ser utilizada de modos constructivos y para extenderse, utilizarse y nutrirse mediante estrategias educativas y normativas.
Falla al resolver o tratar de resolver conflictos de valores personales ética y legalmente.	Se concentra en el proceso y en la ley para la resolución de conflictos, confiando posiblemente también en la ética situacional.	Trata de resolver conflictos de valores personales de modo ético y legal y lo hace sin sacrificar su integridad.

Se guía por la atribución de una mentalidad primaria de coerción, arreglo y competencia despiadada.	Se guía por una trama imperfecta de atribuciones de una mentalidad primaria y secundaria.	Se guía por atribuciones de mentalidad secundaria de búsqueda de consenso, cooperación y colaboración.
Juega con la información o bien la retiene o distorsiona a fin de circunvenir la ley, o los designios de la legislación. Oculta la información requerida a otros funcionarios del gobierno. Oculta la infromación al público o a cualquiera que posea un derecho legítimo para acceder a la misma.	Adopta diversos enfoques según las circunstancias.	Es honesto y sincero al comunicar información, y solo la retiene cuando legal o éticamentne resulta necesa- rio.
Se desinteresa por saber lo que en verdad ocurre, o por comprender lo que hace falta hacer a n de proteger o servir al interés público.	No se compromete a servir al interés público en el buen sentido de la palabra. Se desinteresa por el conocimiento y entendimiento necesarios para maximizar los valores predominantes, la ciencia o el proceso en sí mismo.	Se compromete a servir al interés público. Actúa de modo de poder maximizar los valores de la vida, la salud y las libertades individuales y sociales.
Se mofa de las decisiones judiciales, de los derechos constitucionales, de los derechos humanos, de los valores humanos. Pasa todo ello por alto.	Se muestra e eficazmente indiferente a los derechos humanos y constituciona- les.	Actúa de acuerdo con la ley y con los derechos constitucionales y humanos.
Actúa de modo tal que niega, descuida o minimiza los valores de la vida, la salud y la libertad.	Actúa eficazmente de modo de negar, descuidar o minimizar los valores de la vida, la salud o la libertad.	Actúa de acuerdo con el interés público. Se desenvuelve de modo de poder maximizar los valores de la vida, la salud y las liberta- des individuales y sociales.

		Basa sus acciones en un firme interés por las libertades individuales y sociales.
Descuida o desvaloriza la libertad.	Desatiende o devalúa y socava la libertad con mucha eficacia.	
Lleva a cabo programas, presta servicios, encara problemas sociales pobre e inhumanamente, de modo ineficaz y científico con valores neutros (in a *value neutral scientistic way*, de modo que derrocha recursos humanos, naturales y/o fiscales y materiales. en consecuencia, la ciencia y la tecnología perjudican los propósitos humanos y se encaran como propósitos en sí mismos.	Dirige o ejecuta programas, presta servicios, encara problemas sociales, como si se guiara por valores comerciales predominantes de productividad y humanismo al servicio de la productividad.	Dirige o ejecuta programas, presta servicios, encara problemas les de un modo humano y bondadoso, eficazmente, con sensibilidad, de modo tal de poder conservar los valorados recursos humanos, natur les y/o fiscales, y de modo tal que la ciencia y la tecnología sirvan a los propósitos humanos y se empleen de modo humano.
Permite los esfuerzos organizativos por la buropatología en la que el proceso se torna más importante que el propósito, la autoridad más importante que la realidad, la prioridad más importante que la adaptabilidad.	Se encarga de que los esfuerzos organizativos se concentren en el proceso y no en el propósito, interesándose más por maximizar los valores predominantes de negocios que en servir al interés público.	Se ocupa de que los esfuerzos de organización se caractericen por una salud de organización no burocrática, en la cual el propósito, el servicio, la realidad y la adaptabilidad sean más importantes que el proceso, la autoridad, la forma o la prioridad.
Se concentra en los procedimientos de modo de evadir responsabilidades o desbaratar el propósito del procedimiento.	Se concentra más en el proceso que en el propósi- to. Atiende más al proceso de lograr el bien público que al bien público en si mismo.	Se concentra en el propósito, el servicio, la realidad y la adaptabilidad y en servir al interés público.

Permite que las unidades organizativas, los esfuerzos para la implementación de políticas y la regulación se confundan y superpongan de modo tal que vuelve imposible un ejercicio adecuado del gobierno y la resolución de los problemas complejos así como también la satisfacción de las necesidades humanas y sociales.	Permite que la preocupación por el proceso y la estructura obstaculicen la acción que posee un propósito determinado y la resolución o mejora de los complejos problemas sociales.	Organiza de tal modo que el ejercicio del gobierno puede llevarse a cabo bien, con sensibilidad y e eficacia.
Se interesa por el propósito y el servicio. No pone énfasis en la responsabilidad ni en las obligaciones de los funcionarios públicos para cumplir con el interés público.	Presta demasiada atención al proceso, tanta que el proceso puede convertirse en un fin en sí mismo. Se concentra en la participación o descentralización de modo tal de que éstos se tornan fines en sí mismos y conducen hacia la doble-democratización, promoviendo algunos de los procesos integrales para una democracia representativa pero frustrando otros. No toma en cuenta el problema de responsabilidad por las acciones gubernamentales en los funcionarios públicos. Se concentra en los procesos que, según piensa, aseguran la responsabilidad en lugar de la esencia de la responsabilidad y de la función pública en el interés público.	Se asegura de que el propósito y el servicio tengan prioridad por sobre el proceso. Acentúa la responsabilidad y las obligaciones de los funcionarios públicos en el servicio del interés público y proporciona modos para asegurar la responsabilidad.

Dirige el gobierno de modo tal que éste deja de responder al bien común o lo prejudica, o bien es indiferente al bien común, y pone énfasis en asuntos seudopolíticos (intereses propios o de grupos reducidos) o es de valor neutral o bien nihilista (sin valor, propósito o sentido).	Dirige el gobierno de modo tal que deja de responder al bien común en el sentido de que no le preocupa de modo fundamental el bien común.	Dirige el gobierno de modo de que éste sea sensible a las necesidades públicas y de modo de que cumpla con el interés público desenvolviéndose para maximizar los valores de la vida, la salud y las libertades individuales y sociales mientras trata de hacer el mejor uso de los recursos en el logro de estas metas. Pone énfasis en lo político, encara necesidades y pro- blemas humanos y los valores democráticos esenciales para una sociedad libre y para la libertad en el mundo.
No actúa en base a información, entendimiento y conocimiento accesibles, para prevenir la pérdida de vidas y las amenazas a la salud y las libertades. No actúa aún cuando la solución a los problemas sociales esté a su alcance.	No protege, presenta ni fomenta el interés público a través de una indiferencia selectiva hacia todo tipo de información, entendimiento y conocimiento que se refiere a la preservación de los valores humanos y a la solución de problemas humanos.	Se desenvuelve para proteger, preservar y realzar el interés público.
No asume una actitud de administración y responsabilidad para la protección, preservación y aumento de los recursos humanos y naturales.	Asume una actitud de oportunidad pragmática o indiferente.	Asume una actitud de administración y responsabilidad para la protección, preservación y mejoramiento de los recursos humanos y naturales.

Se encuentra ausente la capacidad para enfrentar crisis o prevenirlas y evitarlas antes de que surjan y tampoco desarrolla tal capacidad.	Implícitamente, no posee dirección, es nihilista, sin metas a largo plazo, por lo general sustenta su incrementalismo desarticulado no interesado en ninguna meta general de desarrollo.	Desarrolla la capacidad para hacer frente a las crisis y para evitarlas antes de que surjan. Es conducente a un gobierno orientado hacia un cambio y desarrollo saludable, en el cual aquellos que integran el gobierno actúan como agentes de cambio y de solución de los problemas sociales.
No responde a las protestas públicas que manifestan que el gobierno no está sirviendo al interés público.	Se concentra en el proceso de ser sensible y responder a los problemas pero no se compromete a servir al interés público.	Es sensible a aquellos de dentro y fuera del gobierno que sienten que se está perjudicando al interés público.

5.3 - The view of Mercosul Legal Systems on ethics

Juan Bautista and Juan de Dios Cincunegui elaborated a precious list of duties, prohibitions and incompatibilities for public agents that we transcribe, due its clarity and practicality.

a) la preservación del estado de derecho;

b) el respeto de los derechos humanos (civiles, sociales, culturales, económicos y políticos);

c) velar por la vigencia del orden jurídico institucional, y contra la usurpación del poder político;

d) anteponer el respeto a la ley y al interés público a los intereses propios y de otros, e inspirar sus decisiones y comportamiento en el cuidado del interés público confiado;

e) excusarse de intervenir en todo asunto que pueda dar lugar a interpretaciones de parcialidad o concurra incompatibilidad moral;

f) demostrar la máxima disponibilidad en sus relaciones con los particulares, permitiendo el pleno ejercicio de sus derechos,

g) asegurar, en el cumplimiento de sus tareas, la paridad de trato entre los ciudadanos y extranjeros que tomen contacto con los mismos en el ejercicio de tareas o funciones a su cargo;

h) velar por la transparencia de su accionar y el resguardo de la confianza de la ciudadanía en las instituciones del Estado;

"toda norma jurídica sea ella justa o injusta, pretende establecer o establece un deber jurídico. (...) uno puede perfectamente decir que en la Alemania nazi la SS tenía el deber jurídico de aprehender a los judíos y enviarlos a los campos de concentración (...) Pero en el sentido real y absoluto de lo que de humano tiene el término deber', como apelación a una conciencia libre, tal deber, así sólo se llame "jurídico" y no moral. (..) "Los individuos deben comportarse como la norma lo estipula" (...) en todos estos casos se siente, se cree que el derecho debe ser obedecido (...) La Alemania nazi, el pueblo en general, los miembros de las SS, los jueces y juristas en general, tenían la convicción (...) ese derecho que ordenaba prisiones, torturas y muertes era y debía ser cumplido."

Prohibiciones Generales e incompatibilidades.

Debería encontrarse prohibido para todo agente público:

a) el ejercicio o soporte de influencias indebidas;

b) la realización de pactos extraoficiales sobre remuneraciones irregulares;

c) la negligencia manifiesta u omisiones graves en el cumplimiento de deberes funcionales;

d) participar en la adopción de decisiones o en actividades que puedan involucrar - directa o indirectamente-, intereses económicos o de cualquier otra índole propios, de parientes o convivientes, de amigos íntimos o de terceros con los que mantenga una vinculación interesada de la que pueda presumirse parcialidad;

e) negar o acordar injustificada y arbitrariamente a algunos prestaciones que sean normalmente acordadas o denegadas a otros en las mismas circunstancias;

f) dar prioridad injustificadamente a la atención de los asuntos de unos en desmedro de otros;

g) permitir o silenciar las irregularidades en que pudieren incurrir las personas que ejerciten funciones, prerrogativas o potestades públicas;

h) aceptar, efectuar o tener en cuenta, en caso que puedan influir sobre el desarrollo de un procedimiento, examen o concurso público, recomendaciones o señalamientos, o cualquier otra forma de intento de influenciar decisiones, a favor o en contra de participantes o interesados;

i) adoptar, en caso de que aspiren a una promoción, traslado u otra medida relativa a su carrera, comportamientos tendientes a influenciar a aquellos que deben o pueden tomar la decisión correspondiente o influenciar sobre la misma, ni pedir a otros que lo hagan;

j) ser proveedor de los organismos del estado donde desempeñen sus funciones, cuando de ellos dependa directa o indirectamente la correspondiente contratación;

k) ser miembro de directorios o comisiones directivas, acreditarse como representante, gerente, apoderado, asesor técnico o legal, patrocinante o empleado de empresas privadas que se rijan por concesiones, o cualquier otra forma de adjudicación prevista en los reglamentos de la administración, otorgadas por el estado Nacional, algún estado provincial o municipio, y que tengan por esa razón, vinculación permanente o accidental con los poderes públicos;

i) participar de cualquier forma o prestar servicios – dentro de los tres (3) años de haber cesado en su cargo – a una persona física o de existencia ideal cuyos intereses hubiesen estado en la esfera de su competencia como funcionario;

ii) realizar para sí o por cuenta de terceros, gestiones ten- dientes a obtener el otorgamiento de una concesión de la admi- nistración pública nacional, provincial o municipal, hasta tres (3) años después de su egreso de la función y bene ciarse directa o indirectamente con la misma;

l) efectuar o patrocinar para terceros, trámites o gestiones administrativas, se encontraren o no directamente a su cargo, hasta tres (3) años después de su egreso de la función;

m) recibir directa o indirectamente beneficios originados en contratos, concesiones o franquicias que celebre u otorgue la administración en el orden nacional, provincial o muni- cipal;

n) mantener vinculaciones que le signifiquen beneficios u obligaciones con entidades directamente fiscalizadas por el organismo o entidad en la que se encuentre prestando servi- cios;

ñ) realizar con motivo o en ocasión del ejercicio de sus funciones, actos de propaganda, proselitismo, coacción ideológica o de otra naturaleza, cualquiera fuese el ámbito donde se realicen las mismas;

o) recibir para sí, familiares o convivientes, dádivas, obsequios o cualquier otro tipo de regalo con motivo o en ocasión del desempeño de sus funciones. en el caso en que los obsequios sean de uso social, cortesía o de costumbre diplomática, deberán ser registrados con fecha, nombres del donante y donatario, valor y motivación. en todos los casos deben ser declarados y pasar al patrimonio del estado cuando excedan de un monto determinado, el que debería ser de nido por la reglamentación; y

p) recibir cualquier tipo de ventaja con motivo u ocasión de sus funciones, así como aprovechar la función para obtener beneficios de cualquier naturaleza.

As a tool to give to our reader the knowledge of the organization of ethics in Mercosur, we now present tables that we elaborate, the content of which is the organization of comparative legislation within the member countries of the bloc.

5.4 - Código de éÉica de la Función Pública – Argentina

Lei - decreto 41/99	Princípios Gerais
Não há a designação específica de código de Etica na Argentina e, sim, "Ley de Ética de La Funcion Publica".	Articulo 2 - Los sujetos comprendidos en esta ley se encuentran obligados a cumplir con los siguientes deberes y pau- tas de comportamiento ético:
Ley 25.188 Ley de Etica de La Funcion Publica Buenos Aires, 29 de septiembre de 1999	a) cumplir y hacer cumplir estrictamente la constitución Nacional, las leyes y los reglamentos que en su consecuencia se dicten y defender el sistema republicano y democráticode gobierno;
Boletin Oficial, 01 de Noviembre de 1999 vigentes	

Decreto Nacional 164/99 (B.o. 7-1-00)	b) desempeñarse con la observancia y respeto de los principios y pautas éticas establecidas en la presente ley: honestidad, probidad, rectitud, buena fe, y austeridad republicana;
	c) velar en todos sus actos por los inte- reses del estado, orientados a la satisfacción del bienestar general, privilegiando de esa manera el interés público sobre el particular;
	d) No recibir ningún bene cio personal indebido vinculado a la realización, retardo u omisión de un acto inherente a sus funciones, ni imponer condiciones especiales que deriven en ello;
	e) Fundar sus actos y mostrar la mayor transparencia en las decisiones adoptadas sin restringir información, a menos que una norma o el interés público claramente lo exijan;
	f) Proteger y conservar la propiedad del estado y sólo emplear sus bienes con los nes autorizados. abstenerse de utilizar información adquirida en el cumplimiento de sus funciones para realizar actividades no relacionadas con sus tareas oficiales o de permitir su uso en benficio de intereses privados;
	g) abstenerse de usar las instalaciones y servicios del Estado para su beneficio particular o para el de sus familiares, allegados o personas ajenas a la función oficial, a fin de avalar o promover algún producto, servicio o empresa;

5.5 - Brazilian legislation on ethics in Federal Public Administration (Inpired on The Inter-American Convention Against Corruption[IACAC]

Codes and Laws (Source: www.plan-alto.gov.br)	General Principles
Decree N° 4.081/2002, establishes the Code of Conduct Ethics for Public Officials in the Presidency and Vice Presidency of the Republic.	I - make it clear that the exercise of professional activity in the Presidency and Vice Presidency of the Republic is a rare distinction from the public agent, which presupposes adherence to the specific ethical norms of conduct provided for in this Code; II - establish the rules of conduct inherent to the exercise of office, job or function in the Presidency and vice-presidency of the republic; III - preserve the image and reputation of the public agent whose conduct is in accordance with the norms established in this code; IV - avoiding the occurrence of situations that may give rise to conflicts between the private interest and the public functions of the public agent; v - create a consultation mechanism, designed to enable prior and prompt clarification of doubts regarding the ethical correction of specific conduct; V - give greater transparency to the activities of the Presidency and vice presidency of the republic.
Decree N° 7.203/2010 - Provides for the prohibition of nepotism within the federal public administration. Binding Formula 13 The appointment of a spouse, partner or relative in a direct line, collateral or by a third party, including the nominating	Art. 2. For the ns of this decree it is considered: i - organ: a) the Presidency of the republic, comprising the vice-presidency, the civil house, the Personal Cabinet and the special advisory; b) the organs of the Presidency of the Republic commanded by a Minister of State or equivalent authority; and c) Ministries;

or servant authority of the same juristic person invested in management, cheer or advisory, for the exercise of a position in a commission or commission, or even a function of direct or indirect public administration in any of the powers of the union, states, Federal District and Municipalities, including adjustment by reciprocal designations, violates federal Constitution. - Date of Approval Plenary Session of August 21, 2008 Source of Publication dje no 162 de 29/8/2008, p. 1.dou de 29/08/2008, p. 1. Legislative Reference Federal Constitution of 1988, art. 37, "caput."	II - entity: autarchy, foundation, public company and mixed economy company; and iii - family member: the spouse, partner or relative in a direct or collateral line, by inbreeding or birth, up to the third degree.
Explanatory Memorandum n° 37, of 18.8.2000, approved on 21.8.2000 code of conduct of the following federal administration.	Art. 1°. The Code of Conduct of Federative Senior Management is hereby established, with the following qualifications: I - to clarify the ethical rules of conduct of the authorities of the Federal High Public Administration, so that society can assess the integrity and smoothness of the governmental decisionmaking process; II - to contribute to the improvement of the ethical standards of the Federal Public Administration, based on the example given by the authorities of higher hierarchical level; iii - preserve the image and reputation of the public administrator whose conduct is in accordance with the ethical norms established in this Code; (...) IV - to establish basic rules on contents of public and private interests and limitations on professional activities subsequent to the exercise of public office;

Decree n° 1.171/994 - Approves the Code of Professional Ethics of the civil servant of the Federal Executive Power.	**Section of deontological rules** I - dignity, decorum, zeal, zeal, and conscience of moral principles are the highest priorities that should guide the public servant, whether in the exercise of office or function, or outside it, since it will re- of the state's own power. their acts, behaviors and attitudes will be directed towards the preservation of the honor and tradition of public services. II - the public servant can no longer despise the ethical element of his conduct. thus, it will not have to decide only between the legal and the illegal, the just and the unjust, the convenient and the inconvenient, the opportune and the inopportune, but mainly between the honest and the dishonest, according to the rules contained in art. 37, caput, and § 4, of the Federal constitution. III - the morality of the public administration is not limited to the distinction between good and evil, but it must be added that m is always the good common. the balance between legality and status in the conduct of the public servant is that it may consolidate the morality of the administrative act. IV - the remuneration of the public servant is borne by taxes paid directly or indirectly by all, even by himself, and therefore, it is required, in return, that administrative morality is integrated in law, as an indissociable element of its application and of its nality, and, as a consequence, erected as a factor of legality.

5.6 — Código de Ética de la Función Pública/Paraguay

Paraguay	General Principles
	El Manual de Ética Pública se encuentra dividido en dos grandes partes: en la Primera Parte, se fundamenta conceptualmente el ejercicio de la función pública desde una perspectiva ética, pero no desde el discurso filosófico, sino desde un enfoque sociológico y antropológico que la entiende desde su dimensión jurídica y cultural.
En Paraguai no hay específicamente un código de Ética, mas existe normativa aplicable en punto a la ética pública, a nivel constitucional y legal.	
HAY, TODAVÍA, EL MANUAL DE ÉTICA PÚBLICA AL DE ÉTICA PÚBLICA CÓMO INCORPORAR LA ÉTICA PÚBLICA EN LA CULTURA INSTITUCIONAL DE L TURA INSTITUCIONAL DE LOS ORGANISMOS Y ENTIDADES DEL ESTADO.	La Segunda Parte plantea la metodología general para la implantación de la gestión ética en los organismos y entidades públicas, y desagrega los pasos metodológicos en los procedimientos necesarios para realizar las construcciones y actividades requeridas. Asimismo, presenta elementos que permiten comprender y gestionar las eventuales resistencias al cambio que se puedan generar a lo largo del proceso de implementación.
	Divorcio entre ley, cultura y ética
	En la administración pública es aceptado que la eficiencia y la transparencia en la gestión pública son resultado de la actuación congruente de los funcionarios públicos dentro de los marcos regulatorios formales e informales, en donde la ley constituye el entorno normativo explícito que basado en la cultura y en la ética,

expresa el interés común; la cultura regional, local y del grupo social al que pertenece el servidor público, por su parte, expresa formas concretas de pensar, sentir y actuar frente al mundo, que no deben entrar en antagonismo con los principios y fines constitucionales y legales sobre el carácter de la función pública, sino por el contrario, ilustra los procedimientos más idóneos para atender las necesidades de la población de acuerdo con su idiosincrasia; y los valores y principios éticos que porta el servidor público, a su vez, regularán sus actuaciones en el marco de la cultura y el cumplimiento de la ley, como mecanismo de autocontrol para orientar sus actuaciones en la búsqueda del bien común y la defensa del interés social sobre el interés particular. (...)

5.7 - Legislation on ethics in the public service in Uruguay

Uruguay	General Principles
En uruguay no hay específicamente un código de Ética, mas existe normativa aplicable en punto a la ética pública, a nivel constitucional y legal.	- Respect
	- Impartiality
- Destacamos la serie: "Manuales de capacitación" N° 1 – Montevideo 2009– junta de transparencia y Ética Pública, del cual se extrae lo siguiente:	- Rectitude
- "La constitución establece en el artículo 58 que "en los lugares y horas de trabajo queda prohibida toda actividad ajena a la función".	- Suitability,
	- Responsibility of public officials.

J. J. de Aréchaga expresó que "es un principio elemental de disciplina administrativa que no necesita ser proclam- ado ni por texto legal ni constitucional".

- El artículo 59, a su vez, establece "la base fundamental de que el funcionario existe para la función y no la función para el funcionario".

- La ley 17.060 de 23 de diciembre de 1998 contiene disposiciones relacionadas con la materia. su ámbito orgánico está inte- grado por todas las entidades estatales y por las personas de derecho público no es- tatales. el ámbito subjetivo es el de todos quienes ejercen un cargo o cumplen una función en esas instituciones. explicita los principios de respeto, imparcialidad, rectitud, e idoneidad.

- A nivel reglamentario el decreto 500/991 al referirse a la responsabilidad de los fun- cionarios públicos consagra el derecho al respeto a la honra, el reconocimiento de su dignidad y las garantías del debido pro- ceso. Por su parte el decreto 30/003 del 23 de enero de 2003 reglamenta y ordena las normas de conducta de la función pública (artículos 8 a 23).

5.8 - Legislation on ethics in the public service in Venezuela

Venezuela	General Principles
Law - Decree 41/99	h) observar en los procedimientos de contrataciones públicas en los que in- tervengan los principios de publicidad, igualdad, concurrencia y razonabilidad; i) abstenerse de intervenir en todo asunto respecto al cual se encuentre comprendi- do en alguna de las causas de excusación previstas en la ley procesal civil.

> CAPITULO III régimen de declaraciones juradas (artículos 4 al 11)
>
> CAPITULO V - incompatibilidades y conflicto de intereses (artículos 13 al 17)
>
> CAPITAL VI - Régimen de obsequios a funcionarios públicos (artículo 18)

CÓDIGO DE ÉTICA PARA EL FUNCIONARIO PÚBLICO / VENEZUELA

Artículo 1°. - Corresponde a los funcionarios públicos:

1. Salvaguardar en todo momento y en cada una de sus actuaciones, los intereses generales del estado y en la preservación del patrimonio público.

2. Actuar con estricto apego a las leyes y a todas las demás normas e instrucciones que deben regir su comportamiento en la realización cabal de todas las tareas que tenga asignadas.

3. Dedicar todos sus esfuerzos para cumplir, con la máxima e ciencia y la más alta eficacia, la misión que le esté encomendada.

4. Realizar permanentemente actividades de superación personal y de colaboración en el mejoramiento institucional de la administración pública y, en particular, del organismo donde preste sus servicios.

5. Rehusar confirma inequívoca el mantenimiento de relaciones o de intereses, con personas u organizaciones, que sean incompatibles con sus cargos y con las atribuciones y funciones que le estén asignadas.

6. Proceder con objetividad e imparcialidad en todas las de- cisiones que le corresponda tomar y en los asuntos en los que deba intervenir.

7. Rechazar en cualquier caso y circunstancia y no solicitar jamás, ni para sí mismos ni para terceros, pagos, bene cios o privilegios en ocasión de los servicios que deba prestar.

8. Ajustar su conducta, de modo estricto y sin excepciones, a favor de la transparencia en la administración pública manteniendo la confidencialidad y reserva de información en aquellos casos excepcionales cuya divulgación esté prohibida, por razones del superior interés público, de modo expreso y temporal.

9. Denunciar ante la autoridad competente y rechazar cualquier actividad contraria al correcto manejo de los fondos y del interés público.

10. Tratar a los ciudadanos y a los funcionarios públicos con absoluto respeto y con apego a la estricta legalidad, prestándole sus servicios y colaboración de manera e ciente, puntual y pertinente, sin abusar en modo alguno de la autoridad y atribuciones que le sean conferidas en ocasión del cargo que desempeñe.

Artículo 2°.- Se exhorta a todos los funcionarios públicos a ajustar su conducta, en el desempeño de sus funciones, a las normas señaladas en el artículo anterior.

Comuníquese y publíquese EDUARDO ROCHE LANDER Comptroller General of the Republic.

Source: http://www.anticorrupcion.gov.ar/25.188.PdF.acesso 16.01.2013.

The study of comparative law that we carry out has the capacity to prove that there is symmetrical legislation on ethics both at the international and national levels.

The unification of the legislation as we have been proposing, with the creation of an specialized administrative justice in Mercosur, can certainly turn the fight against corruption more efficient, provides more efficacy to governments efforts, and become paradigm to the world.

CHAPTER 6

White Collar Crimes - An International Concern

Odete Maria Oliveira asserts that time is a witness of the migration of crimes against the person to crimes against property, from the passing of a blood crime to a crime of fraud.

Here is an excerpt from what Oliveira says (2003: 43):

> "Michel Foucault sums up:" In fact, the passage from a criminality of blood to a criminality of fraud is part of a complex mechanism, in which the development of production, increase of wealth, a greater legal and moral valorization of property relations, stricter surveillance method, narrower policing of the population and better-tuned techniques of discovery and capture of information."

The structuring of the democratic state of law has given rise to other categories of crimes, which are treated as lesser offensive potential by the law. The truth, however, is that acts of corruption with public property, money and income, cause daily as much or more impact as the crime of genocide.

Corruption assaults the public treasury that is the source of funding for public policies. This is why educating citizen and the public official should be considered public policy.

Ketan J. Patel (2007: 80) says with propriety that sustainable change can not be implemented without a change of mentalities.

Heres comes a lesson of Juan carlos Ferré olivé (2002: 74) about white collar crimes:

> "The globalization of crime has accompanied the globalization of the economy. Using the global media that allow an instantaneous circulation / intervention in the financial markets and having brilliant advisors, both jurists and economists, very well-to-do people in different countries, almost always as exemplary professionals and citizens above any suspect, criminal organizations play with the differences of the various administrative-criminal systems, leapfrogging from country to country, and diverting the white goods to where detection becomes more difficult or where corruption more easily solves the problem.
>
> Money laundering and corruption are the faces of the same coin, the Siamese brothers of the same mother, and it is not an exaggeration that most of the money laundering activities are carried out through corrupt practices.
>
> The corruption settled in. It is Faria Costa who uses the expression "culture of corruption" that effectively characterizes the way of being and living today, where profit is god and the "economic ratio" has assumed the nature of the highest value, to which ethics and law must be subordinated, and perhaps, in the future, freedom itself."

Eduardo A. Fabián Capakrós, Professor of "Derecho Penal de la Universidad de Salamanca/España", cited by Olivé (2002: 103) demonstrates the worldwide concern with the white collar crime:

> "Junto con el fenómeno de la delincuencia organizada, el blanqueo de capitales y la corrupción constituyen los núcleos temáticos sobre los que se ha volcado la mayor parte de los esfuerzos realizados en el marco internacional. Entidades tales como las Naciones Unidas (NU), el Consejo de Europa (CE), la Unión Europea (UE), la Organización de Estados Americanos (OEA), la Organización para la Cooperación y

el Desarrollo Económico (OCDE), etc., se han preocupado de ofrecer vías de solución a estos problemas, tal vez viejos en su esencia, pero dotados hoy, en el marco de la «aldea global», de un significado que desconoce precedentes."

6.1 - Concept of white collar crime

Brazilian Law 9.613/1998 defines white-collar crime (corporate crimes) as the transformation of illicit assets into licit assets.

The doctrine, in turn, offers several concepts of the white-collar crime, as Olivé informs

> "Whitening, washing, reconverting, legitimizing, legalizing money or goods are synonymous expressions that translate the same reality-process by which one intends to give a lawful appearance to proceeds from illicit activities. All these acts that constitutes a process, can be made up of innumerable and successive operations, tending towards an increasing difficulty in identifying their origin, whether due to their temporal, geographical or economic distance, or their integration into legal economic circuits.

> The option of the Portuguese legislator for the term "laundering", despite the popular usage, does not seem to me to be happy, based on the black-white opposition, as an image of the good / bad, pure / impure or lawful / illicit. It is obviously a metaphorical adaptation, as well as the expressions "money laundry" or "reciclagio de dinaro sproco". In fact, there is no white or black money, clean or dirty, pork or baked, perfumed or foul smelling. Pecunia non olet, said the Vespasian emperor, in imposing the tax on latrines.

Money is money, and is acquired either lawfully or
illegally, in which case, like other goods of similar origin,
there is a need for money laundering."

Julio E.S. Virgolini (2004: 9-10), discussing the origin of the conception
introduced by Edwin Sutherland as crimes committed by non-members of
the popular classes, thus clarifies:

"El primer jalón de estos esfuerzos se volcaron sobre un
conjunto de fenómenos que, en un momento histórico, se dio
en llamar "delitos de cuello blanco" o "white collar crime".

Aunque en términos estrictamente sociológicos el término
tuvo amplia difusión a través de una investigación
ya clásica de Charles WRIGHT MII.I.S referida a la
estructura de la sociedad estadounidense y al papel de sus
clases medias, su empleo en el ámbito de la criminología
fue anterior y se debe a la obra de otro sociólogo, Edwin
Sutherland, quien lo aplicó por primera vez en este campo
en su famosa disertación pronunciada en diciembre de
1939 ante la Sociedad Americana de Sociología.

Bajo ese término se delimitó conceptualmente un
horizonte de investigación criminológica hasta entonces
desconocido o escasamente transitado: una categoría de
delitos cuya fenomenología presenta rasgos diferentes o
distinguibles de aquellos que tradicionalmente habían
constituido el objeto de la disciplina y que, por oposición
a la especificidad de los delitos de cuello blanco, pueden
clasificarse dentro del amplio y difuso género de la
criminalidad común o convencional.

Más allá de las discusiones sobre la definición precisa y los alcances
del nuevo concepto, de lo que nos ocuparemos más adelante, conviene
adelantar de manera provisoria que éste se refiere al fenómeno delictivo
protagonizado por la clase de más elevado nivel socioeconómico,
caracterizado éste por su respetabilidad, por su estatus social o, alternativa
o conjuntamente, por el rol ocupacional desplegado en ocasión del delito.

De todas maneras, lo que era claro y, además, era novedoso para la época, está constituido por un dato negativo: delito de cuello blanco era el que no tenía como autores a los integrantes de las clases populares."

6.2 - Pillars or Grounds of White Collar Crime

Juan Carlos Ferré Olivé (2002: 235) says that on the other hand, this transnational organized crime is essentially based on four pillars.

These are the four pillars Ferré cites:

1– financing, inter alia, trafficking in narcotic drugs, weapons and human beings;
2– intensive use of new communication and information technologies;
3– the profitability / enhancement of the gains obtained through money laundering and investment in new forms of operations, as well as in traffic and corruption; and
4– image laundering, socio-economic credibility and the search for respectability by members of the governing bodies of these organizations.

6.3 - The legal good guarded in the crime

The crime, for the finalist theory of action is any typical and unlawful action. His study presupposes the existence of an active and passive subject, of objective and subjective elements, of leading commands and accessory commands.

White-collar crime affects the socio-economic order and the administration of justice in the victimized country, as emphasized by LIVÉ (2002: 77):

"And it is possible to emphasize on the subject four positions: a) the same juridical asset of the previous crime; b) the socio-economic order; c) the administration of justice; d) two or more legal assets, constituting a pluri-offensive crime. Fernandes Godinho, indicates "the state's interest in confiscation the profits of crime", a value that does not seem to me to be autonomous, since it integrates the good administration of justice."

6.4 - White collar crime relationship with corruption

Every crime is a form of corruption and white-collar crime or corporate crime does not escape this truth. As Sutherland has said, this kind of crime is bound up with both the poor and the rich. In this work interestes us, especially those white-collar crimes related to the Public Administration and, therefore, that involves public officials directly or in partnership with those citizens who offers bribery or any kind of illegal benefits.

Juan Carlos Ferré olivé says that corruption involves a movement of capital that escapes the control of organs and entities, including those of control, and that the proceeds of the activities of white-collar criminals, sooner or later, ends up within the financial system where money is washed and recycled.

Ferré Olivé concludes that the corruption of civil servants and public authorities is one of the great problems of our time. This is what he says:

> "CORRUPTION involves important movements of money which escape the watchfulness of the administrative and jurisdictional entities in control. e product of the criminal activities sooner or late ends up inside the financial and banking system once that money has been properly laundered or recycled. It is because of this that an integral fight against corruption can not ignore the activities of money laundering which are related to corruption performed by public functionaries and authorities.
>
> (...)
>
> III - Money laundering and corruption
>
> The corruption of public officials and authorities is one of the great problems of our time. This phenomenon, which

affects the rich world and the poor world alike, generates extraordinary income for those responsible, who must necessarily rejoin the "legal" economic circuit for their enjoyment. This is where the criminal figure of money laundering is particularly important."

July E.S. Virgollini (2004: 50,53) in his work *Crímenes excelentes: Delitos de Cuello Blanco, crimen organizado y corrupción,* gives us a masterful lesson on the links between money laundering and corruption:

"Some valuations regarding the provisions contained in the OECD convention on bribery of foreign public officials in international commercial transactions (1997).

1474/5000

Indeed, in a clear synthesis of the most usual positions regarding crime, SUTHERLAND argues that:

Because these cases are concentrated in the low socioeconomic class, the theories about criminal behavior have given great importance to poverty as a cause of crime or other social conditions and personal traits that are associated with poverty. The assumption in these theories is that criminal behavior can be explained only by pathological factors, whether social or personal. The social pathologies that have been underlined are poverty, and related to it, poor housing, the lack of organized recreation, lack of education and the breakdown of family life.

The personal pathologies that have been suggested as explanations of criminal behavior were, first, biological abnormalities; When research studies questioned the validity of these biological explanations, the next explanation was intellectual inferiority and recently emotional instability.

Some of these scholars believed that personal pathologies were inherited and were the cause of poverty, as well as of criminal behavior, while others believed that personal pathologies were caused by poverty and the pathological conditions associated with poverty, and that this personal pathology contributed to the perpetuation of poverty and related social pathologies.

His thesis is:

... that these social and personal pathologies are not an adequate explanation of criminal behavior (...) that people of the upper socio-economic class participate in a lot of criminal conduct.

This behavior will be different from that which corresponds to the low socio-economic class, but not in its essential characteristics but basically in the administrative procedures used in the treatment of offenders; Obviously, this type of social differences will no longer be decisive or important from the point of view of the causation of crime, since "the signicative of the crime of 'white collar' is that it is not associated with poverty, or with pathologies social and personal problems that accompany poverty".

(...)

2. Is white collar crime a crime?

2. 1. The positive thesis of Sutherland

In this section we propose to examine one of the most important arguments that has given rise to the problem of white collar crime: the relativity of its criminal character.

For this we have denominated it with the title used by Sutherland in an article of 1945, to sustain his conviction that the facts that faced in his study constituted true crimes. His thesis was against the current opinion - both in the field of public opinion and in academic circles - which argued that criminal behavior could not in any way be attributed to behaviors that are proper or habitual in the area of business and that when they are observed naturally, they are isolated from the social reproach caused by true (conventional) crimes.

(...)

In short, his opinion is clearly aimed at agreeing criminal character to the so-called "white collar crime": the behaviors considered within that category respond to the two requirements that ordinarily satisfy the concept of crime, that is, the legal prohibition of an act as socially harmful and the predetermination of a sanction."

6.5 - White collar crimes legislation in Mercosur Public Administrations

ARGENTINA	Ley 26.388 - Modificación. sancionada: junio 4 de 2008 Promulgada de hecho: junio 24 de 2008 El Senado y Cámara de Diputados de la Nación Argentina reunidos en Congreso, etc. sancionan con fuerza de Ley:
	Articulo 1° incorpóranse como últimos párrafos del artículo 77 del código Penal, los siguientes: el término "documento" comprende toda representación de actos o hechos, con independencia del soporte utilizado para su jación, almacenamiento, archivo o transmisión.
	(...)
	CODIGO PENAL

ARTICULO 5° — incorpórase como artículo 153 bis del código Penal, el siguiente: Artículo 153 bis: será reprimido con prisión de quince (15) días a seis (6) meses, si no resultare un delito más severamente penado, el que a sabiendas accediere por cualquier medio, sin la debida auto- rización o excediendo la que posea, a un sistema o dato informático de acceso restringido.

La pena será de un (1) mes a un (1) año de prisión cuando el acceso fuese en perjuicio de un sistema o dato informático de un organismo público estatal o de un proveedor de servicios públicos o de servi- cios financieros.

más severamente penado, el que a sabiendas accediere por cualquier medio, sin la debida auto- rización o excediendo la que posea, a un sistema o dato informático de acceso restringido.

La pena será de un (1) mes a un (1) año de prisión cuando el acceso fuese en perjuicio de un sistema o dato informático de un organismo público estatal o de un proveedor de servicios públicos o de servi- cios nancieros.

ARTICULO 6° — sustitúyese el artículo 155 del código Penal, por el siguiente: ARTÍCULO 155: será reprimido con multa de pe- sos un mil quinientos ($ 1.500) a pesos cien mil ($ 100.000), el que hallándose en posesión de una correspondencia, una comunicación electrónica, un pliego cerrado, un despacho telegrá co, telefó- nico o de otra naturaleza, no destinados a la publi- cidad, los hiciere publicar indebidamente, si el he- cho causare o pudiere causar perjuicios a terceros. está exento de responsabilidad penal el que hubie- re obrado con el propósito inequívoco de proteger un interés público.

ARTICULO 7° — sustitúyese el artículo 157 del código Penal, por el siguiente: ARTÍCULO 157: será reprimido con prisión de un (1) mes a dos (2) años e inhabilitación especial de un (1) a cuatro (4) años, el funcionario público que revelare hechos, actuaciones, documentos o datos, que por ley deben ser secretos.

ARTICULO 8° — sustitúyese el artículo 157 bis del código Penal, por el siguiente: artículo 157 bis: será reprimido con la pena de prisión de un (1) mes a dos (2) años el que:

1. A sabiendas e ilegítimamente, o violando sis- temas de con dencialidad y seguridad de datos, accediere, de cualquier forma, a un banco de da- tos personales;

2. Ilegítimamente proporcionare o revelare a otro información registrada en un archivo o en un banco de datos personales cuyo secreto estuviere obligado a preservar por disposición de la ley.

3. Ilegítimamente insertare o hiciere insertar da- tos en un archivo de datos personales. cuando el autor sea funcionario público sufrirá, además, pena de inhabilitación especial de un (1) a cuatro (4) años.

ARTICULO 9° — Incorpórase como inciso 16 del artículo 173 del código Penal, el siguiente: inciso 16. el que defraudare a otro mediante cualquier técnica de manipulación informática que altere el normal funcionamiento de un sistema informático o la transmisión de datos.

ARTICULO 10. — Incorpórase como segundo pár- rafo del artículo 183 del código Penal, el siguiente: en la misma pena incurrirá el que alterare, destruyere o inutilizare datos, documentos, pro- gramas o sistemas informáticos; o vendiere, dis- tribuyere, hiciere circular o introdujere en un sistema informático, cualquier programa desti- nado a causar daños.

(...)

ARTICULO 12. — sustitúyese el artículo 197 del código Penal, por el siguiente: artículo 197: será reprimido con prisión de seis (6) meses a dos (2) años, el que interrumpiere o entorpeciere la comunicación telegrá ca, te- lefónica o de otra naturaleza o resistiere violen- tamente el restablecimiento de la comunicación interrumpida. (...)

| **BRAZIL** | Law N° 9.613 / 1998. |
| | |

Decree n° 2.799 / 1998 (by abstract) - Provides for crimes of "laundering" or concealment of goods, rights and values; the prevention of the use of the financial system for the crimes established in this Law; creates the Financial Activities Control Council - COAF, and makes other arrangements.

THE PRESIDENT OF THE REPUBLIC
I hereby announce that the National Congress decrees and I sanction the following Law:

CHAPTER I
Of the crimes of "Washing" or concealment of Goods, rights and values.

(Art. 1) to conceal or conceal the nature, origin, location, disposition, movement or ownership of goods, rights or values arising, directly or indirectly, from a criminal offense. (wording given by Law no. 12.683, of 2012)

Penalty: imprisonment, from three (3) to ten (10) years, and fine. (wording given by Law No. 12,683 of 2012)

§ 1° incorrenamesmapenaquem, in order to prevent the use of assets, rights or values derived from criminal offenses: (wording given by Law 12.683, of 2012)

I - converts them into lawful assets;

II) acquires, receives, exchanges, negotiates, gives or receives them in guaranty, custody, holds, moves or transfers;

III - imports or exports goods with values that do not correspond to true values.

§ 2° incurs, also, in the same penalty who: (wording given by Law no. 12.683, of 2012)

I - uses, in economic or financial activity, goods, rights or valuations of financial compensation; (drafting of Law No. 12,683 of 2012)

II - participates in a group, association or office having knowledge that its main or secondary activity is directed to the practice of crimes foreseen in this Law.

§ 3° The attempt is punished in terms of the sole paragraph of art. 14 of the Criminal Code.

§ 4°. The penalty shall be increased from one to two thirds if the crimes of nests in this Law are committed repeatedly or through a criminal organization. (wording given by Law No. 12,683 of 2012)

§ 5°, the penalty may be reduced from one to two thirds and be served in an open or semi-open regime, allowing the judge to stop applying it or replace it at any time with a restrictive penalty of rights if the author, coauthor or participant spontaneously cooperates with the authorities, providing clarifications that lead to the determination of criminal offenses, identification of authors, coauthors and participants, or the location of assets, rights or values that are the object of the crime. (wording given by Law No. 12,683 of 2012)
(...)
Art. (4) The judge, ex officio, at the request of the Public Ministry or by means of a representation of the police officer, after hearing the Public Prosecution Service within twentyfour (24) hours, if there are indications of a criminal offense, may decree assets, rights or values of the investigated or accused, or existing in the name of interposed persons, who are the instrument, product or benefit of the crimes provided for in this Law or of previous criminal infractions. (wording given by Law No. 12,683 of 2012)

Paragraph 1. Provision shall be made for the early alienation to preserve the value of the assets whenever they are subject to any degree of deterioration or depreciation, or when there is a timetable for their maintenance. (wording given by Law No. 12,683 of 2012)

	Paragraph 2. The judge shall determine the total or partial release of the assets, rights and values when proven lawful of their origin, maintaining the constriction of the necessary assets, rights and values and are aware of the compensation of damages and payment of cash benefits, fines and costs arising from the criminal offense. (wording given by Law No. 12,683 of 2012) Paragraph 3. No request for release shall be known without the personal appearance of the accused or of the person concerned referred to in the caput of this article, and the judge may determine the practice of acts necessary for the preservation of goods, rights or values, without prejudice to the provisions of § 1o. (wording given by Law No. 12,683 of 2012) Paragraph 4. Securing measures on property, rights or values may be ordered to compensate for the damages resulting from the previous criminal infraction or that provided for in this Law or for payment of pecuniary benefit, fine and costs. (wording given by Law No. 12,683 of 2012)
PARAGUAY	LEY NO 2523, EL CONGRESO DE LA NACION PARAGUAYA SANCIONA CON FUERZA DE LEY: QUE PREVIENE, TIPIFICA Y SANCIONA EL ENRIQUECIMINETO ILICITO EN LA FUNCION PUBLICA Y EL TRAFICO DE INFLUENCIAS (abstract) Artículo 1°.- Objeto de la Ley. La presente Ley tiene por objeto tipificar y sancionar el enriquecimiento ilícito en la función pública y el tráfico de influencias. Artículo 2°.- Ambito de su aplicación. esta Ley será aplicable a toda persona que cumpla una función pública, o tenga facultades de uso, custodia, administración o explotación de fondos, servicios o bienes públicos, cualquiera sea la denominación del cargo, o su forma de elección, nombramiento o contratación, que incurra en los hechos punibles tipificados en la presente Ley.

Artículo 3°.- Enriquecimiento ilícito.

1) Comete hecho punible de enriquecimiento ilícito y será sancionado con pena privativa de libertad de uno a diez años, el funcionario público compren- dido en cualquiera de las situaciones previstas en el artículo 2°, quien con posterioridad al inicio de su función, incurra en cualquiera de las siguientes situaciones:

a) Haya obtenido la propiedad, la posesión, o el usu- fructo de bienes, derechos o servicios, cuyo valor de adquisición, posesión o usufructo sobrepase sus legí- timas posibilidades económicas, y los de su cónyuge o conviviente.

b) Haya cancelado, luego de su ingreso a la función pública, deudas o extinguido obligaciones que afectaban su patrimonio, el de su cónyuge o su conviviente, y sus pa- rientes hasta el segundo grado de consanguinidad y de a nidad, en condiciones que sobrepasen sus legítimas posibilidades económicas.

2) Será aplicable también a los casos previstos en el inciso 1) de este artículo, la pena complementaria prevista en el artículo 57 del código Penal.
(…)

artículo 7°.- Tráfico de influencias.

1) El que reciba o se haga prometer para sí o para un tercero, dinero o cualquier otro bene cio como estí- mulo o recompensa para mediar ante un funcionario público, en un asunto que se encuentre conociendo o haya de conocer invocando poseer relaciones de importancia o in uencia reales o simuladas, será castigado con pena privativa de libertad hasta tres años o multa.

2) Igual pena se aplicará a quien entregue o prometa dinero o cualquier otro bene cio, para obtener el fa- vor de un funcionario público.

(…)

3) Si la conducta señalada en los incisos 1) y 2) de este artículo estuviera destinada a hacer valer una in uencia ante un magistrado del Poder judicial o ante scales del Ministerio Público, a n de obtener la emisión, dictado, demora u omisión de un dicta- men, resolución o fallo en asuntos sometidos a su consideración, el límite legal máximo de la sanción se elevará hasta cinco años de pena privativa de libertad.

Artículo 8°.- Administración en provecho propio.

1) Será castigado con pena privativa de libertad hasta diez años, el funcionario público que decida, autorice o suscriba actos o contratos administrativos que otorguen, en forma directa, beneficios indebidos Paraguai para su provecho personal, o para su cónyuge o conviviente, o el de sus parientes hasta el segundo grado de consanguinidad o segundo de afinidad.

URUGUAY	La república Oriental del Uruguay con fecha 22 de noviembre de 1998 dictó la ley 17.016 que reprimía, al igual que lo hacía el artículo 25 de la ley 23.737 argentina, el lavado de dinero en el marco de la lucha contra el narcotráfico. Posteriormente, ley No 17.343 extendió la aplicaci- ón de los tipos penales contenidos en los artículos 54 a 57 de la ley de estupefacientes cuando el objeto material de la operación de lavado fuesen bienes, productos o instrumentos provenientes de delitos vinculados a las siguientes actividades: terrorismo; contrabando superior a U$S 20.000 (veinte mil dólares); tráfico ilícito de armas, explosivos, municiones o material destinado a su producción; trá co ilícito de órganos, tejidos y medicamentos; trá co ilícito de hombres, mujeres o niños; extorsión; se- cuestro; proxenetismo; trá co ilícito de sustancias nucleares; trá co ilícito de obras de arte, animales o materiales tóxicos. La ley 17.016 incorporó a la legislación uruguaya las siguientes figuras delictivas: 1) financiar actividades relacionadas con el narco- trá co (art. 32); 2) convertir o transferir bienes, productos o instru- mentos del delito y sus sustitutos (art. 54);

3) adquirir, poseer, utilizar, tener en su poder o re- alizar cualquier tipo de transacción sobre bienes, productos o instrumentos originarios o subrogados provenientes de los delitos mencionados (art. 55);

4) ocultar, suprimir, alterar los indicios del delito (art. 56);

5) impedir la determinación real de la naturaleza, el origen, la ubicación, el destino, el movimiento o la propiedad reales de tales bienes, o productos u otros derechos relativos a los mismos (art. 56).

6) asistir al o a los agentes de la actividad delicti- va, ya sea para asegurar el beneficio o el resultado de tal actividad, para obstaculizar las acciones de la justicia o para eludir las consecuencias jurídi- cas de sus acciones, o prestarle cualquier ayuda, asistencia o asesoramiento (art. 57).

La prevención del lavado de activos está a cargo de: la Prosecretaría de la Presidencia de la re- pública; el centro de capacitación en materia de Lavado de activos; el Ministerio de economía y Finanzas; y el Banco central de uruguay del que dependen las superintendencias supervisoras de todos los sectores y la unidad de información y análisis Financiero (UIAF); la Policía dependien- te del Ministerio del interior y la Prefectura Na- val dependiente del Ministerio de defensa.

2) Será aplicable también a los casos previstos en el inciso 1) de este artículo, la pena complementaria prevista en el artículo 57 del código Penal.
(...)

artículo 7°.- Tráfico de influencias.

1) El que reciba o se haga prometer para sí o para un tercero, dinero o cualquier otro bene cio como estí- mulo o recompensa para mediar ante un funcionario público, en un asunto que se encuentre conociendo o haya de conocer invocando poseer relaciones de importancia o in uencia reales o simuladas, será castigado con pena privativa de libertad hasta tres años o multa.

La ley establece para las entidades la obligación de identificación de clientes, conservación de la información, obligación de comunicar las ope- raciones e identificar a los clientes de las tran- sacciones en efectivo por valor superior a 10.000 dólares.

La UIAF es el receptor de oda esa información; se halla ubicada dentro de la superintendencia de instituciones de intermediación Financiera y cuenta con el apoyo financiero y técnico del Ban- co central.

VENEZUELA	(abstract)
	(La ley que sigue Aprobada en Primera Discusión el 04 de octubre del 2016 y, por lo tanto, muy recientemente):
	LEY CONTRA LA CORRUPCIÓN Y PARA LA SALVAGUARDA DEL PATRIMONIO PÚBLICO
	EXPOSICIÓN DE MOTIVOS DE LA LEY CONTRA LA CORRUPCIÓN Y PARA LA SALVAGUARDA DEL PATRIMONIO PÚBLICO
	Los cambios sociales, económicos y políticos en las sociedades contemporáneas se suceden cada vez con mayor velocidad dada la extensión de los efectos de la era de la información y la globalización. La actividad criminal en tanto que fenómeno social también muta con rapidez, lo que genera una necesidad creciente de actualización y de constante adecuación de los ordenamientos jurídicos a fin de brindar al Estado y a la sociedad los medios más efectivos y garantistas para combatirla.
	La corrupción en sentido lato es uno de estos fenómenos que evoluciona constantemente para evadir los controles que se han dispuesto a fin de garantizar la confianza pública en las instituciones. Tal circunstancia demanda la revisión periódica de los instrumentos normativos destinados a prevenir y combatir su flagelo.

En Venezuela tal adaptación resulta imperativa dada la extensión de esta perniciosa práctica y también debido al crecimiento exponencial del sector público por la incorporación de personas y órganos que tradicionalmente se encontraban fuera de la estructura del Estado y sin manejo de recursos públicos como organizaciones no gubernamentales, las instancias y expresiones organizativas del Poder Popular, entre otras, que ahora participan en la formulación, ejecución, evaluación y control las políticas públicas.

En ese sentido, la corrupción en sentido amplio ha incidido en el paulatino desmejoramiento de las funciones propias de los entes y órganos del Estado venezolano, así como en la afectación del Patrimonio Público de tal modo que el Estado se ve impedido de garantizar los más esenciales derech os de la población, fenómeno que ha sido especialmente relevante en las dos últimas décadas.

Siendo éste último un elemento relevante, en virtud de encontrarnos ante grandes hechos de corrupción cuya responsabilidad no ha logrado ser determinada por el sistema de justicia venezolano, evidenciando de esa manera grandes cantidades de bienes, recursos públicos y demás activos que han sido extraídos de la Nación de manera ilícita, y cuyo destino se ha visto disipado ante terceros, personas interpuestas y entidades bancarias pertenecientes a los llamados paraísos fiscales.

La evolución legislativa en materia contra la Corrupción ha de ser progresiva, es por ello que ha resultado ineludible implementar en el cuerpo normativo de esta Ley, una serie de elementos necesarios para la efectiva y eficaz consonancia de esta materia específica con los demás instrumentos de carácter sustantivo y adjetivo de nuestro ordenamiento jurídico.

En ese sentido, se implementan los conceptos de ética pública y moral administrativa, en referencia a la conducta que deben mantener los funcionarios públicos en el desempeño de sus funciones, con preeminencia de los intereses del Estado, sobre el interés particular, fundamentado en los principios constitucionales que rigen la Administración Pública y se considera corrupción, además del daño al patrimonio público, el incumplimiento de esta ley y otras normas que rigen el comportamiento del funcionario público, o de cualquier otra persona natural o jurídica, pública o privada, nacional o extranjera que contrate con el Estado o reciba, administre o custodie sus bienes y recursos públicos.

Para salvaguardar el patrimonio público se incorpora la condición de funcionarios públicos hasta administradores o directores, particulares, y a quienes corresponda la administración y ejecución de recursos transferidos a los consejos comunales, comunas, organizaciones socioproductivas y demás instancias y expresiones organizativas del Poder Popular, provenientes de fondos públicos, para un ejercicio fiscal.

Además se considera patrimonio público aquel que corresponda a las fundaciones y asociaciones civiles y demás instituciones creadas con fondos públicos; que reciban fondos públicos para su funcionamiento, o que sean dirigidas por las personas de los órganos y entidades del Poder Público nacional, estadal, de los distritos y distritos metropolitanos, del Poder Público municipal y de las demás entidades locales, en los territorios y dependencias federales, institutos autónomos nacionales, estadales, distritales y municipales, el Banco Central de Venezuela, las universidades públicas y demás personas de Derecho Público nacionales, estadales, distritales y municipales.

Con el fin de asignar responsabilidades en el marco de la lucha contra la Corrupción, se hace expresa la mención de los consejos comunales, comunas, organizaciones socioproductivas y demás instancias y expresiones organizativas del Poder Popular como sujetos activos y pasivos de la Ley, estableciendo dentro de la noción de lo que se considera patrimonio público, a los recursos que cualquiera de los entes u órganos del sector público asigne a estos particulares, que se considerarán funcionarios públicos, a los solos efectos, de las regulaciones y sanciones, que establece esta Ley.

Con el objeto de establecer una autoridad que se encargue de notificar a la Contraloría General de la República del nombramiento o designación, así como el cese de funciones, de las personas que administren los recursos asignados por cualquier ente u organismo público, a los efectos de la ejecución de proyectos para la comunidad, se implementa una norma que obliga a la Comisión Electoral de los Consejos Comunales a ejercer dicha función.

Se estableció un capítulo referido a los principios para prevenir la corrupción y salvaguardar el patrimonio público, y se crea la norma exige a los funcionarios públicos, rendir cuenta por la utilización de pasajes y viáticos, otorgados por el ente u órgano, para las gestiones inherentes a sus funciones, bajo pena de incumplimiento.

Fue incorporada la norma que obliga a los funcionarios públicos que en el desempeño de sus funciones contraten con personas naturales o jurídicas, a verificar la información legal, técnica y financiera, de los mismos, en el Registro Nacional de Contratistas.

En aras de fortalecer la lucha contra la Corrupción, fortalecer la ética pública y la moral administrativa y evitar las posibles situaciones de conflicto de intereses que pudieran surgir en el ejercicio de las funciones de los funcionarios públicos, se establece un capítulo con una serie de normas destinadas a evitar que se antepongan los intereses de naturaleza particular ante los intereses delEstado acarreando responsabilidades civiles, penales y administrativas en caso de verificarse situaciones de conflicto de intereses.

Atendiendo a las recomendaciones de la Convención de las Naciones Unidas Contra la Corrupción, se implementa la Declaración Jurada de Intereses, como una de las medidas para prevenir el conflicto de intereses, respecto a los deberes que compete a los funcionarios públicos y en los casos que aplique, a los particulares. Esta declaración, al igual que la declaración jurada patrimonio, deberán presentarla las personas incluidas en el artículo 3 de esta ley, dentro de los treinta días siguientes a la toma de posesión del cargo, y dentro de los treinta días posteriores al cese del ejercicio del mismo; y consiste en la indicación tanto a la Contraloría General de la República, como al superior jerárquico, de las actividades profesionales y económicas, que desarrolla distinta a la función pública que desempeña, con el objeto de garantizar la transparencia de sus actuaciones, por cuanto se deslindan de su función pública aquellas actividades que pueda desarrollar el funcionario público fuera de su jornada de trabajo, con recursos privados, produzcan o no renta o beneficio monetario, todo lo cual propende a evitar la contraposición de los intereses particulares con el interés público, es decir conflicto de intereses.

En virtud de la facultad constitucional de representar al Estado en el ejercicio del poder punitivo y llevar a cabo la titularidad del ejercicio de la Acción Penal, el Ministerio Público podrá exigir la declaración jurada de patrimonio, la declaración jurada de intereses y la declaración del impuesto sobre la renta a las personas obligadas a formularlas, quienes permitirán a los funcionarios competentes su inspección así como los libros, cuentas bancarias, documentos, facturas y otros elementos que comprueben el contenido de las mismas.

Se crea la norma que establece la obligación para la Contraloría General de la República de mantener un registro automatizado y actualizado, con la información sobre las denuncias, procedimientos y sanciones administrativas impuestas a los funcionarios públicos, y de remitir a solicitud del Ministerio Público dicha información, con motivo de las investigaciones que realicen.

Se establecieron responsabilidades a las Máximas Autoridades respecto de la obligación de identificar los vehículos, naves y aeronaves oficiales asignados a los órganos o entes bajo su dirección, con la finalidad de evitar la utilización distinta a las propias del órgano o ente al que se encuentra asignado el referido vehículo. Existiendo además una pena corporal para quienes utilicen dichos vehículos, naves y aeronaves para fines distintos a las labores oficiales del órgano o ente. Con lo que se establece de esa manera la responsabilidad, tanto de las Máximas Autoridades como de quienes utilicen ilegalmente los vehículos, agravándose dicha responsabilidad cuando los fines sean políticos o electorales.

Asimismo se establece el aumento de las penas en los delitos previstos en el Título VII a fin de aplicar el Principio de Proporcionalidad que viene consagrado universalmente desde el siglo XVIII, acogido como parte del concepto de equidad y justicia, cuyo máximo exponente fue César Beccaria en su obra "De los Delitos y las Penas", publicado en 1764, así como Montesquieu lo dejó asentado en su obra "Del Espíritu de las Leyes", quien sostenía que éstas tienen un carácter preventivo en sentido general frente a la sociedad.

En relación a los obstáculos que se presentan en los procedimientos e investigaciones que se siguen a los supuestos responsables de delitos contra la corrupción, se incorpora la norma que obliga a gerentes, directivos y responsables de entidades bancarias y empresas aseguradoras así como a los notarios públicos, registradores y cualquier persona natural o jurídica que no suministre la información requerida por parte del Ministerio Público y La Contraloría General de la República, en relación a la verificación patrimonial de la declaración jurada de patrimonio o la comisión de los delitos previstos en esta ley, acarreando en caso de incumplimiento una pena corporal.

Se incorpora como delito, la Omisión de Comprobantes, por parte de los funcionarios públicos, en los cuales deben demostrar la inversión de los fondos públicos bajo su administración.

Con respecto a los delitos del sector privado, se establecen nuevas formas delictivas referentes al soborno cuando se realiza, por cualquier persona, en el curso de actividades económicas, financieras o comerciales, obteniendo un beneficio indebido que redunde en su provecho propio o el de otro cuando realice o se abstenga de actuar faltando al deber inherente de sus funciones. Estableciendo de esa manera la penalización de conductas relacionadas con la corrupción, que no son realizadas por funcionarios públicos ni que afectan directamente el patrimonio público.

Se consagra el delito de Blanqueo de Bienes producto de delitos de corrupción, para cualquier persona que se beneficie, oculte o disimule el origen ilícito de los bienes producto de delitos de corrupción o que ayude a eludir las consecuencias jurídicas relacionadas con tales hechos. De igual forma se sanciona a quien oculte o disimule la naturaleza, el origen, la ubicación, la disposición, el movimiento o la propiedad de bienes, a sabiendas que son producto de la corrupción.

En aras de agravar aquellas conductas relacionadas con el nepotismo o circunstancias que constituyan conflicto de intereses, se establece una disposición de agravantes genéricas cuando los delitos estipulados en el Capítulo II del Título VII,

sean cometidos por las máximas autoridades jerárquicas o para favorecer o beneficiar a su cónyuge, concubino, o parientes dentro del cuarto grado de consanguinidad o segundo de afinidad; o a las personas jurídicas en las cuales su cónyuge, concubino, o parientes dentro del cuarto grado de consanguinidad o segundo de afinidad tengan o hayan tenido participación en los últimos cinco (5) años.

Se implementa una disposición relacionada con la Cooperación Jurídica Internacional, en aras de fortalecer los mecanismos judiciales y administrativos de las instituciones venezolanas, quienes respecto de autoridades extranjeras podrán solicitar información necesaria para las investigaciones, aplicación de medidas preventivas, confiscación de bienes y solicitudes de extradición, estableciendo de esa manera elementos que permitan fortalecer la cooperación internacional en la lucha contra la corrupción.

Como elemento novedoso, este cuerpo normativo introduce la figura de la Cooperación Eficaz, como un mecanismo que permite a aquellos sujetos involucrados en la comisión de los delitos tipificados en esta Ley, a disminuir la pena que resultare aplicable, cuando suministren datos o información precisa, verídica y comprobable siempre que conduzca al esclarecimiento de los hechos; la comisión de delitos; la identificación de los presuntos responsables, la ubicación y destino de los recursos, bienes y demás activos extraídos de manera ilícita del patrimonio público, siempre que dicha información esté vinculada con delitos de mayor o igual gravedad de los que se investiga. Estableciendo además el beneficio de la extinción de la acción penal a aquellas interpuestas personas que estén dispuestas a reintegrar los recursos, bienes o demás activos que fueron extraídos, ocultados o disimulados de manera ilícita a través de su persona.

LEY CONTRA LA CORRUPCIÓN Y PARA LA SALVAGUARDA DEL PATRIMONIO PÚBLICO
TÍTULO I
DE LAS DISPOSICIONES FUNDAMENTALES
Capítulo I
De las disposiciones generales

Objeto

Artículo 1. La presente Ley tiene por objeto promover la educación contra la corrupción y los valores de ética pública y moral administrativa en los ciudadanos; establecer las normas que deben observar las personas sujetas a la misma para la administración, manejo o custodia de los bienes públicos, a fin de salvaguardar el patrimonio público y garantizar su adecuada utilización conforme a los principios de honestidad, probidad, participación, transparencia, eficiencia, eficacia, legalidad, rendición de cuentas y responsabilidad que rigen el ejercicio de la función pública; así como la tipificación de los delitos contra el patrimonio público y el correcto funcionamiento de las instituciones del Estado y las sanciones que deberán aplicarse a quienes infrinjan estas disposiciones.

Ámbito subjetivo de aplicación

Artículo 2. Están sujetos a esta Ley los funcionarios públicos; los consejos comunales, comunas, organizaciones socioproductivas y demás instancias y expresiones organizativas del Poder Popular y, las demás personas naturales o jurídicas, públicas o privadas en los términos establecidos en esta Ley.

Funcionarios públicos

Artículo 3. Sin perjuicio de lo que establezca la Ley que regula el Estatuto de la Función Pública, y a los solos efectos de las regulaciones y sanciones previstas en esta Ley, se consideran funcionarios públicos a:

Quienes estén investidos de funciones públicas, permanentes o transitorias, remuneradas o no, originadas por elección, por nombramiento, designación o contrato, otorgado por la autoridad competente, al servicio de la República, de los estados, de los territorios y dependencias federales, de los distritos, de los distritos metropolitanos, de los municipios, así como de los institutos autónomos nacionales, estadales, distritales o municipales, de las universidades públicas, del Banco Central de Venezuela o de cualesquiera de los órganos o entes que ejercen el Poder Público.

Los directores, administradores, empleados y obreros de las sociedades civiles y mercantiles, fundaciones, asociaciones civiles, cooperativas, cajas de ahorro y demás formas asociativas e instituciones en las que alguno de los órganos o entes de los señalados en el artículo 4 de esta Ley tengan, separada o conjuntamente, participación igual o mayor al cincuenta por ciento (50%) del capital social; constituidas o dirigidas por alguno de tales órganos o entes o con recursos públicos; o en las cuales tales órganos o entes designen sus autoridades o directivos; o cuando los aportes presupuestarios o contribuciones efectuadas en un ejercicio presupuestario, por una o varias de las personas antes mencionadas representen el cincuenta por ciento (50%) o más de su presupuesto o patrimonio.

Los voceros o integrantes de los consejos comunales, comunas, organizaciones socioproductivas y demás instancias y expresiones organizativas del Poder Popular.

Las personas naturales o jurídicas que en cualquier forma contraten, negocien o celebren operaciones con cualesquiera de los órganos o entes mencionados en los numerales anteriores o que reciban aportes, subsidios, otras transferencias o incentivos fiscales, o que en cualquier forma intervengan en la administración, manejo o custodia de bienes y recursos público.

Cualquier otra persona en los casos previstos en esta Ley.

Las disposiciones de la presente Ley, se aplican a las personas indicadas en este artículo, aun cuando cumplan funciones o realicen actividades fuera del territorio de la República.

A los efectos de esta Ley, las expresiones funcionario público, empleado público, trabajador público y servidor público tendrán un mismo y único significado.

Patrimonio público

Artículo 4. Se considera patrimonio público aquel que corresponde por cualquier título a:

Los órganos y entes a los que incumbe el ejercicio del Poder Público Nacional.

Los órganos y entes a los que incumbe el ejercicio del Poder Público Estadal.

Los órganos y entes a los que incumbe el ejercicio del Poder Público en los distritos y distritos metropolitano.

Los órganos y entes a los que incumbe el ejercicio del Poder Público Municipal y las demás entidades locales, previstas en la Ley Orgánica del Poder Público Municipal.

Los órganos y entes a los que incumbe el ejercicio del Poder Público en los territorios y dependencias fede

Los institutos autónomos nacionales, estadales, distritales y municipal.

El Banco Central de Venezuela.

Las universidades públicas.

Lasdemás personas de derecho público nacional

estadales, distritales y municipal.

Las sociedades de cualquier naturaleza en las cuales las personas a que se refieren los numerales anteriores tengan participación en su capital social; así como las que se constituyan con la participación de ésta.

Las sociedades civiles y mercantiles, fundaciones, asociaciones civiles, cooperativas, cajas de ahorro, fondos y demás instituciones constituidas con recursos públicos, o que sean dirigidas por las personas a que se refieren los numerales anteriores, o en las cuales tales personas designen sus autoridades; o cuando los aportes presupuestarios o contribuciones efectuadas en un ejercicio presupuestario, por una o varias de las personas a que se refieren los numerales anteriores representen el cincuenta por ciento (50%) o más de su presupuesto.

Se considera igualmente patrimonio público, los recursos entregados a particulares, consejos comunales, comunas o cualquier otra instancia o expresión organizativa del Poder Popular, por los órganos o entes del sector público mencionados en los numerales anteriores, mediante transferencias, aportes, subsidios, contribuciones, créditos o alguna otra modalidad similar para el cumplimiento de finalidades de interés o utilidad pública, hasta que se demuestre el logro de las finalidades para las cuales fueron otorgados. Las personas que administren tales recursos estarán sometidas a lo establecido en esta Ley, y a las demás Leyes que rijan la materia.

"The cartels as the most serious injury to the competition and general aspects of its combat in Brazil. Cartel is an explicit or implicit agreement between competitors to manipulate price or production quotas and share their customers and market. Cartels are the most serious harm to competition and harm to consumers by raising prices and restricting supply, making goods and services more expensive or unavailable."

"The cartels as the most serious injury to the competition and general aspects of its combat in Brazil. Cartel is an explicit or implicit agreement between competitors to mainly price or production quotas, customer and market share markets. Cartels are the most serious harm to competition and harm consumers by raising prices and restricting supply, making goods and services more expensive or unavailable."

We note, for last, that Brazil has Law 9.613 / 1998, which provides for the crimes of "laundering" or concealment of goods, rights and values; the prevention of the use of the financial system for illicit activities provided for therein. Also creates the board of control of financial activities - COAF.

In Brazil, we also have Law 8.429 / 92, which deals with acts of impropriety practiced by public agents and private individuals, against the Public Administration.

The summary of this record is that if the political-juridical class of Mercosur or any other country apply the existing laws, there will be an impressive reduction in corruption with public assets, money and revenues, because it is a fact that we do not change culture without a changing of mentality.

The issues we need to address are:

Who is interested in combating corruption in Brazil?

Who is interested in combating corruption within Mercosur member countries?

Who cares about corruption in the world?

CHAPTER 7

Existence of Law against Corruption in the Mercosur, afert Approval of the Inter-American Convention Against Corruption - IACAC

The comparative study that we conducted shows that the members of Mercosur have normative acts with specific reference and rules to combat corruption with public funds.

In Brazil, Law no. 8.112 / 90 mentions corruption in its art. 132, paragraph XI, but can not be considered a specific law to combat such practice, since it deals with the legal regime of federal public servants.

Law No. 12.846 / 2013, also known as the Anticorruption Law, represents an important advance in providing for objective liability, in the civil and administrative field, of companies that practice acts that are harmful to the national or foreign public administration.

We present below comparative tables on the existence of specific anticorruption laws in the scope of Mercosur Public Administration.

7.1 - Comparative tables of Mercosur member countries, on specific law to combat corruption

ARGENTINA	Approval of the new law 27.401 of Criminal Liability of Legal Persons in crimes committed against public administration. This law was promoted by the National Executive Power - through the Anticorruption Office - and published in the Official Gazette on December 1, 2017. Effective March 2, 2018.
	The Anti-Corruption Office (OA) celebrated the approval of the Law on Corporate Criminal Liability in the Chamber of Deputies.
	Until now, the Argentine legal system only provided that individuals could be sanctioned or punished for committing corruption offenses.
	With this legislation, Argentina will measure up to other countries in the region and the world, such as Chile, Brazil, Colombia, Mexico, the United States, Spain and France. It will also comply with international commitments made upon ratification of the OECD Transnational Bribery Convention. Argentina was the only one of the 41 signatory countries that did not have it.
	The objective of the regime sanctioned by the Chamber of Deputies is to fight corruption through the generation of incentives (sanctions and mitigation of them for having integrity standards) so that legal persons implement integrity programs and cooperate with the authorities.
	It also provides for the possibility of entering into collaboration agreements with legal entities in exchange for information in order to identify the natural persons who committed the crimes, both in the private sector and in the public sector.
	In addition, the law increases penalties for corruption offenses and allows the Argentine justice system to judge crimes committed by Argentine companies abroad.

Based on this initiative, the OA will establish guidelines and guidelines to regulate integrity programs in the private sector and implement the obligation of state suppliers to have these anti-corruption programs.

The sanction of this law, whose project was mentioned by the president of the Nation Mauricio Macri, at the opening of the 135th period of ordinary sessions this year, had been sent to Congress in October 2016.

The main changes introduced are:

• Go back to the original project in that only corruption offenses are included in the law. They are: "Bribery and influence peddling, national or transnational"; "Negotiations incompatible with the exercise of public functions," Concussion "(illegal exactions)," Illicit enrichment of officials and employees" , and "Balance and false reports aggravated".

• Establish the creation of an integrity program to prevent corruption within the company.

• Hold companies accountable for the crimes committed by the people who work there. The fine can only be exempted if these three requirements are met: the company must self-sue in the courts; he must have a program of integrity adequate to the requirements of the law and he must return the benefit of the crime.

• Establish that the fines will be two to five times the profit obtained illegally by the company.

• Prohibit for ten years from participating in state competitions or bids for companies and the dissolution of trade union status when it was created for the sole purpose of committing crimes, among other sanctions, for companies that are found guilty.

• Incorporate SMEs.

• Promote "effective collaboration agreements", where the legal entity can commit to the Public Prosecutor's Office to collaborate and provide "accurate, useful and verifiable data for the clarification of the facts.

"Fuente: https://www.argentina.gob.ar/noticias/se-sanciono-la-ley-de-responsabilidad-penal-empresaria-en-casos-de-corrupcion. Acess in Oct 31,2018.

BRAZIL	Law No. 12,846 / 2013, also known as the Anti-Corruption Law, represents an important advance in providing for the objective accountability, in the civil and administrative sphere, of companies that practice acts harmful to the national or foreign public administration.

In addition to meeting international commitments assumed by Brazil, the law closes a breach in the country's legal system by directly addressing the conduct of corruptors. The Anti-Corruption Law provides for penalties as an administrative fine - up to 20% of the gross turnover of the company - and the leniency agreement instrument, which allows damages to be recovered faster, in addition to investigative leverage.

The Ministry of Transparency and General Comptroller of the Union (CGU) is responsible for a large part of procedures such as the establishment and trial of administrative processes of accountability and conclusion of leniency agreements within the scope of the Federal Executive Branch.

Objective Responsibility: companies can be held accountable in cases of corruption, regardless of the verification of fault.

More rigid penalties: the value of fines can reach up to 20% of the gross annual turnover of the company, or up to 60 million reais, when it is not possible to calculate gross billing. In the judicial sphere, even the compulsory dissolution of the legal person can be applied.

Leniency Agreement: If a company cooperates with investigations, it can achieve a reduction in penalties.

Scope: Law can be applied by the Union, states and municipalities and has competence even on Brazilian companies acting abroad.

"Fuente: http://www.cgu.gov.br/assuntos/responsabilizacao-de-empresas/lei-anticorrupcao. Acesso em 31.10.2018.

PARAGUAY	LEGISLATIVE POWER - LAW N° 2535 WHICH APPROVES THE UNITED NATIONS CONVENTION AGAINST CORRUPTION THE CONGRESS OF THE NATION PARAGUAYA SANCTIONS WITH FORCE OF LAW: Article 1.- Approval of the United Nations Convention against Corruption, adopted by the General Assembly of the United Nations, through Resolution No. 58/4, in New York City, United States of America, on March 31 October 2003, and signed by the Republic of Paraguay on December 9, 2003, in the city of Mérida, United States of Mexico, whose text is as follows: "UNITED NATIONS CONVENTION AGAINST CORRUPTION Preamble The States Parties to this Convention, Concerned about the gravity of the problems and threats posed by corruption for the stability and security of societies by undermining the institutions and values of democracy, ethics and justice and by compromising sustainable development and the rule of law, Concerned also about the links between corruption and other forms of crime, in particular organized crime and economic crime, including money laundering,

Concerned also about cases of corruption involving vast amounts of assets, which may constitute a significant proportion of State resources, and which threaten the political stability and sustainable development of those States,

Convinced that corruption has ceased to be a local problem and has become a transnational phenomenon that affects all societies and economies, which makes international cooperation essential to prevent and fight against it,

Convinced also that a comprehensive and multidisciplinary approach is required to effectively prevent and combat corruption,

"Fuente   http://www.hacienda.gov.py/normativa/Ley%202.535-2005%20Que%20aprueba%20la%20Convenci%C3%B3n%20 de%20las%20Naciones%20Unidas%20contra%20la%20 Corrupci%C3%B3n.pdf. Acesso em 31.10.2018.

| URUGUAY | *LEY N° 17060 - LEY CRISTAL - FUNCIONARIOS PUBLICOS*

Promulgación: 23/12/1998 - Publicación: 08/01/1999

CAPITULO VI - ASPECTOS ADMINISTRATIVOS

Artículo 20

Los funcionarios públicos deberán observar estrictamente el principio de probidad, que implica una conducta funcional honesta en el desempeño de su cargo con preeminencia del interés público sobre cualquier otro. El interés público se expresa en la satisfacción de necesidades colectivas de manera regular y continua, en la buena fe en el ejercicio del poder, en la imparcialidad de las decisiones adoptadas, en el desempeño de las atribuciones y obligaciones funcionales, en la rectitud de su ejercicio y en la idónea administración de los recursos públicos.

Artículo 21

Los funcionarios públicos observarán los principios de respeto, imparcialidad, rectitud e idoneidad y evitarán toda conducta que importe un abuso, exceso o desviación de poder, y el uso indebido de su cargo o su intervención en asuntos que puedan beneficiarlos económicamente o beneficiar a personas relacionadas directamente con ellos. Toda acción u omisión en contravención del presente artículo hará incurrir a sus autores en responsabilidad administrativa, civil o penal, en la forma prescrita por la Constitución de la República y las leyes.

Artículo 22

Son conductas contrarias a la probidad en la función pública:

1) Negar información o documentación que haya sido solicitada en conformidad a la ley.

2) Valerse del cargo para influir sobre una persona con el objeto de conseguir un beneficio directo o indirecto para sí o para un tercero.

3) Tomar en préstamo o bajo cualquier otra forma dinero o bienes de la institución, salvo que la ley expresamente lo autorice.

4) Intervenir en las decisiones que recaigan en asuntos en que haya participado como técnico. Los funcionarios deberán poner en conocimiento de su superior jerárquico su implicancia en dichos asuntos, para que éste adopte la resolución que corresponda.

5) Usar en beneficio propio o de terceros información reservada o privilegiada de la que se tenga conocimiento en el ejercicio de su función.

Referencias al artículo

"Fuente http://www.impo.com.uy/bases/leyes/17060-1998. Acessed in 31.10.2018.

VENEZUELA	(I have already presented a table before, about this law)
	(abstract)

(The law that was adopted in First Discussion on October 04, 2016 and, therefore, very recently):

LAW AGAINST CORRUPTION AND FOR PUBLIC HERITAGE SAFEGUARD

EXPLANATORY STATEMENT OF THE LAW AGAINST CORRUPTION AND FOR PUBLIC HERITAGE SAFEGUARD

Social, economic, and political changes in contemporary societies are increasingly occurring given the extent of the effects of the information age and globalization. Criminal activity as a social phenomenon also mutates rapidly, which generates an increasing need for updating and constant adaptation of legal systems in order to provide the State and society with the most effective and guaranteed means to combat it.

CHAPTER 8

Laws of Public Administrations of Mercosur

The rule of law is based on obeying the principle of legality. The public administrations are studied in the context of the Administrative Law. The structure is created by law, its agents governed by law, the competence of each class of public officials is defined by law. That's why nobody is above law and must do what the law says, under the responsibility of abuse or deviation of its purpose. Any deviation of the conduct dictated by law can be understood as cause for a consequence, which normally under the context of the substantive due process of law, is a punishment, or at least, should be.

Just as there is an organic law, that is, one that creates and structure entire body of each of the Mercosur Public Administrations, there are laws governing the relationship between them and their public officials. We present them, in abstract, in the tables below:

ARGENTINA	NATIONAL PUBLIC ADMINISTRATION
	Decree 103/2001
	Approve the National Modernization Plan.
	Bs. As., 25/1/2001
	HAVING SEEN, Law No. 24,156 on Financial Administration and Control Systems of the National Public Sector, Law No. 25,152 on Fiscal Solvency and Quality of Public Expenditure, Law No. 25,344 on Financial Economic Emergency and Decree No. 229 dated March 8, 2000, and

CONSIDERING:

That it is essential that the NATIONAL EXECUTIVE POWER carry out a process of modernization and administrative reform oriented to streamline the functioning of the National Public Administration and to introduce in the management of public organizations the achievement of measurable and quantifiable results.

That Law No. 25,152 establishes the measures to which the powers of the National State must be adjusted for the administration of public resources: the formulation of the General Budget of the National Administration, the efficiency and quality of Public Management, the program of quality assessment of expenditure, multi-year budget, public information and free access.

That the article 5° clause c) of the aforementioned rule establishes and authorizes the CHIEF OF CABINET OF MINISTERS to celebrate program agreements with the executing units of budgetary programs, in order to achieve greater efficiency, effectiveness and quality in their management.

That on the basis of the provisions of the aforementioned article 5 and taking into account the powers granted to the CABINET OFFICER OF MINISTERS, it is necessary to establish the framework of action of the aforementioned program agreements by the CABINET OFFICE OF MINISTERS.

That Article 42 of the NATIONAL CONSTITUTION recognizes the rights that assist consumers and users of goods and services, especially adequate and truthful information, in conditions of equitable and dignified treatment.

That by virtue of Decree No. 229/00, public organizations must provide better services, better provision of information to citizens and guarantee the transparency of their actions.

That in the course of the year 2000 modernization actions were established in organizations such as the FEDERAL ADMINISTRATION OF PUBLIC INCOME (AFIP), the PROMIN, the MINISTRY OF EDUCATION and the ARGENTINE MINING GEOLOGICAL SERVICE (SEGEMAR).

That, it is necessary to generalize the experiences made to the rest of the Organizations of the National Public Administration, aligning said actions to the Agreement-Programs mechanism foreseen in Law No. 25,152.

That this measure is issued in the exercise of the powers conferred by Article 99, paragraph 1, of the National Constitution.

Thus,

THE PRESIDENT OF THE NATION ARGENTINA

DECREE:

Article 1 - The NATIONAL MODERNIZATION PLAN of the National Public Administration, which appears as Annex I to the present, is approved.

(...)

TRANSVERSAL TRANSFORMATIONS

MANAGEMENT OF THE HUMAN CAPITAL

The evaluation of performance on the basis of merit, the recognition of incentives, promotion conditioned by qualification and training and not by seniority, the adoption of salary systems that compensate for merit and responsibility have been only exceptional cases.

Public employment remains vulnerable to political patronage, evaluation minimizes conflict through equalization rather than recognition of merit, promotion operates automatically over time, and wage systems preserve ladder conquests, without criteria that justify regimes and disparate treatments for similar situations.

The public administration has been characterized by a deficit in the management of human resources. The time has come to ensure an adequate integrated management of the human capital of the Administration through the articulation of the various systems that make their effective management in accordance with the guidelines of the new management model and holding agents accountable for their actions and results through mechanisms of incentives.

The National Plan for State Modernization proposes to launch a series of actions that aim to improve the provision of public services and to professionalize and dignify the role of public sector workers.

Lines of work and expected results

• Updating, review and modernization of collective labor agreements that govern the labor relations of the public administration.

• Promotion and incentive of the best agents for their results and separation of those who are not up to their responsibilities.

• Regulation of the current legal regulations (Law N ° 25.164) that regulates labor relations in the national public sector.

• Development of career and professionalization regimes based on merit, transparency, respect for public ethics, equality of opportunities and the growing strengthening of the labor competencies of employees.
Source: http://www.adminpublica.org.ar/ OrganizacionDelEstadoYDeLaAdministracionPublicaNacional. pdf. Acessed in November 2, 2018.

BRAZIL	DECREE-LAW No. 200, OF FEBRUARY 25, 1967.
	It provides for the organization of the Federal Administration, establishes guidelines for Administrative Reform and provides other measures.

THE PRESIDENT OF THE REPUBLIC, using the powers conferred by art. 9, § 2, of the Institutional Act No. 4, of December 7, 1966, decrees:

TITLE I

OF THE FEDERAL ADMINISTRATION

Art. 1° The Executive Power is exercised by the President of the Republic assisted by the Ministers of State.

Art. 2° The President of the Republic and the Ministers of State exercise the powers of their constitutional, legal and regulatory competence with the help of the organs that make up the Federal Administration.

Art. 3 Respected the constitutional competence of the Legislative Power established in Article 46, clauses II and IV of the Constitution, the Executive Power will regulate the structuring, attributions and functioning of the organs of the Federal Administration. (Drafting given by Decree-Law No. 900, of 1969)

Art. 4 The Federal Administration includes:

I - The Direct Administration, which is constituted of the integrated services in the administrative structure of the Presidency of the Republic and the Ministries.

II - The Indirect Administration, which comprises the following categories of entities, endowed with their own legal personality:

a) Authorities;

b) Public loans;

c) Mixed economy companies.

d) public foundations. (Included by Law n° 7.596, of 1987)

Sole Paragraph. The entities included in the Indirect Administration are linked to the Ministry in whose area of competence its main activity is framed. (Renumbered from § 1 by Law No. 7,596, of 1987)

(...)

Art. 5° For the purposes of this law, it is considered:

- I - Autarchy - the autonomous service, created by law, with legal personality, assets and own income, to carry out typical activities of the Public Administration, which require, for its better functioning, decentralized administrative and financial management.

- II - Public Emprésa - the entity endowed with legal personality under private law, with its own assets and exclusive capital of the Union, created by law for the exploitation of economic activity that the Government is forced to exercise by force of contingency or administrative convenience being able to wear any of the forms admitted by law. (Drafting given by Decree-Law No. 900, of 1969)

III - Mixed Economy Company - the entity endowed with legal personality of private law, created by law for the exploitation of economic activity, in the form of a limited company, whose shares with voting rights belong in their majority to the Union or the entity of the Indirect Administration society. (Drafting given by Decree-Law No. 900, of 1969)

- IV - Public Foundation - the entity endowed with legal personality of private law, non-profit, created by virtue of legislative authorization, for the development of activities that do not require execution by organs or entities of public law, with administrative autonomy, patrimony owned by the respective management bodies, and operation financed by Union resources and other sources. (Included by Law n° 7.596, of 1987)

§ 1 In the case of subsection III, when the activity is subject to a state monopoly regime, the majority shareholding will correspond only to the Union, on a permanent basis.

§ 2° The Executive Power will frame the entities of the Indirect Administration existing in the constant categories of this article.

§ 3° The entities dealt with in section IV of this article acquire legal status with the registration of the public deed of their incorporation in the Civil Registry of Legal Entities, the other provisions of the Civil Code concerning foundations do not apply to them. (Included by Law n° 7.596, of 1987)

TITLE II

OF THE FUNDAMENTAL PRINCIPLES

Art. 6 The activities of the Federal Administration obey the following fundamental principles:

I - Planning.

II - Coordination.

III. Decentralization.

IV. Delegation of Competition.

V - Control.

Source: http://www2.planalto.gov.br/. Acessed in November 2, 2018.

PARAGUAY	Norma Number: Law of June 22, 1909
	Date of Promulgation: 1899-01-01

Date of Sanction: 1899-01-01

Title of the Standard: Law of June 22, 1909
of administrative and financial organization of the state

Content of the Standard: LAW OF ADMINISTRATIVE AND
FINANCIAL ORGANIZATION OF THE STATE

Law No. 1/1909

THE SENATE AND CHAMBER OF DEPUTIES OF THE NATION
PARAGUAYA MEETING IN CONGRESS, SANCTION WITH
STRENGTH OF LAW

Art. 1 ° .- The Government provides the expenses of the Nation
with the funds of the National Treasury, formed of the product of
the rights of export and import, sale or lease of public lands, income
from mail, railways, loans and operations of credit and of the other
taxes or contributions that the Congress dictates by special laws
(Article 4 of the National Constitution).

Art. 2 .- The ordinary expenses are considered indispensable and
permanent for the normal course of the Public Administration;
extraordinary, those that are invested in certain objects without
permanent character; and special, those required to pay for
exploitation of government agencies and economic enterprises.

Art. 3 ° .- Ordinary resources are considered those that come directly
from the application of the annual or permanent laws that establish
taxes and contributions; extraordinary those created for a particular
object without permanent character; And special, the arising from the
alienation or sale of government assets and the profits of the agencies
and economic enterprises thereof.

Art. 4 ° .- Every law that authorizes the placement of a loan, must
specify the resources with which the service of the debt should be
made and its amortization.

Art. 5 .- The resources obtained by borrowing may not be applied but to the determined objects that the law must specify. authorize them, under the responsibility of the people who invest them or destine them to other objects.

Art. 6 .- No tax established or increased, to cover the construction of special works may be applied, interim or definitively, to objects other than those determined in the law of its creation, nor last longer than the one used to redeem the debt that is contracted.

Art. 7 - No expense may be made that was not previously authorized by law, except in the case of Article 9 of the Constitution or of facts that matter a public calamity.

Art. 8 ° .- This law and the regulations issued by the Executive Power constitute the basis of the organization of the Budget, the Accounting, the Treasury, Public Credit, acquisitions, the perception and investment of government resources, the account, and its prescriptions must adjust all acts and administrative contracts.

(...)

V

EMPLOYEES

(...)

Art. 177.- The employees and permanent officials of the administration will enjoy the salary assigned by the Budget or special laws and will be entitled to retirements and pensions in accordance with the

Articles 241 et seq.

Art. 178.- The persons who perform functions or commissions accidental will only have the remuneration that the law or the decree of P.E. that dispose of the contingent or reserve funds.

(...)

Art. 180.- The General Accounting Office will keep a book for the consignment of the names and addresses of all public employees and their respective employers, as well as the date of their appointment, possession of the position, leave of absence, retirement and the cause, and will not liquidate any salary or remuneration until they constitute low your signature the address, which will subsist for all purposes as long as it has not been changed in the same way.

Art. 181.- Salaries shall be liquidated from the taking of possession of the charge, and to this effect shall be communicated to the General Accounting Office in the manner provided by the regulations of this law. It will be understood by takes possession of the definitive reception of the position of the person replaced.

Art. 182.- The employees of the General Treasury and those in charge of the guard, conservation, employment and receipt of money, securities, property, income and taxes belonging to the Government, will give, before enter to exercise their functions, bonds to respond to the charges resulting from their administration.

Art. 183.- The bond referred to in the previous article must be a satisfaction of P.E. or of the heads of departments authorized for this purpose and determined in accordance with the regulatory provisions, taking the basis of the nature of the administration and functions that are entrusted and ensuring that responsibility can be made effective easily. The Court of Accounts will review, rate the sufficiency and cancel the bonds in the surrender files of accounts

Art. 184.- The Heads of all administrative departments have power to impose as disciplinary measures the warnings and the fine in accordance with the regulations of this law.

Art. 185.- The amount of the fine imposed for any reason will enter the retirement and pension fund.

Art. 186.- The dismissal decreed in the cases of articles 123 subsection 3 ° and 159 disqualification for the subsequent performance of any administrative position. An appointment occurred in contravention of this article, the General Accounting will observe P.E. the disqualification and will not liquidate any salary to the appointed.

Art. 187.- The employee who obtains permission to work will not enjoy salary. absence for more than eight days, except in the case of illness in which the employee will be entitled to pay up to three months.

Art. 188.- No employee of the Administration may enjoy during the year for more than twenty days of leave not motivated by illness. This period will be extended in exceptional circumstances at the discretion of the P.E. and in case of illness, the duration of the permit will be determined prudentially.

Art. 189.- The power to give permission to administrative employees corresponds to the Heads of offices but three days and three days to the Chiefs superiors up to twenty days, without disease and up to forty for sickness.

Art. 190.- All permission granted will be communicated through the respective distributions to the General Accounting Office.

Art. 191.- Every employee, upon leaving office, shall have the right to ask the General Accounting the testimony of the annotations that in their respect are included in the book established by art. 180.

Source: http://www.hacienda.gov.py/normativa/Ley%201-1909%20De%20 Organizzaci%C3%B3n%20Administrativa%20y%20Financiera%20 del%20Estado.pdf. Acessed in November 2, 2018.

URUGUAY	Law 17,060 SAY NORMS REFERRED TO THE MISUSE OF PUBLIC POWER (CORRUPTION).

The Senate and the House of Representatives of the Oriental Republic of Uruguay, meeting in the General Assembly,

DECREE:

CHAPTER I

Scope of application and definitions

Article 1

This law will be applicable to public officials of:

A) Legislative Power, Executive Power and Judicial Power.

B) Court of Accounts.

C) Electoral Court.

D) Contentious Administrative Court.

E) Departmental Governments.

F) Autonomous Entities and Decentralized Services.

G) In general, all agencies, services or state entities, as well as non-state public persons.

Article 2°.

For the purposes of this law, public officials are the persons referred to in article 175 of the Criminal Code.

Article 3°.

For the purposes of Chapter II of this law, corruption is understood as the undue use of public power or public function, in order to obtain an economic benefit for itself or for another, whether or not the State has been damaged.

CHAPTER II

Advisory Board

Article 4°.

An Advisory Board on Financial Economic Matters of the State is created, whose activities and tasks will be the following:

1) Advise at the national level regarding the crimes foreseen by this law, against the Public Administration (Title IV, excluding Chapters IV and V, of the Penal Code) and against the economy and public finances (Title IX of the Penal Code), which are attributed to any or some of the public officials listed in articles 10 and 11 of this law.

It will be composed of three members, who will last five years in their functions as of their designation by the President of the Republic, acting with the Council of Ministers, with the consent of the Chamber of Senators always granted by three fifths of votes of the total of components, among people of recognized experience and professional and moral solvency.

The President of the Republic, in agreement with the Council of Ministers, may dismiss by a well-founded resolution the members of the Board with the consent of the Chamber of Senators granted by the same majority required for their appointment. If the Senate is not issued within sixty days, the Executive Power may enforce the dismissal.

2) It will have as an exclusive task the advice to the judicial bodies as criminal competence, issuing an opinion within the framework of its subject matter, when the Justice or the Public Prosecutor's Office so decide.

The performance of the Board in the fulfillment of its mission shall be regulated by what is established in Section V, Chapter III, Title VI, Book I of the General Code of the Process, as applicable.

3) Complaints that are made about the commission of crimes included in Chapter I, will be presented before the competent judicial body, or the Public Ministry, which may order the Board to obtain and systematize all the documentary evidence that exist were necessary for the clarification by the Judge of the facts reported.

4) The Board will have sixty days for the fulfillment of the task indicated in the previous section, being able to request the Judge, for only one time, the extension of the term, which will be granted whenever there is enough merit for it, for a maximum of thirty days.

Upon expiration of the term or extension, where appropriate, the Board shall send to the body that legally corresponds to receive the collected information. These will be accompanied by an explanatory report of the correlation of the same with the reported facts.

5) For the fulfillment of its functions, the Board will have the following accessory tasks:

A) Collect, when it deems appropriate, information on the conditions of regularity and impartiality with which public contracts for goods, works and services are prepared, formalized and executed.

B) Receive the sworn statements referred to in articles 10 and following of this law.

C) Determine, at the request of the interested party, if the latter must present the sworn declaration of assets and income referred to in Chapter V of this law.

D) To propose the modifications of norms on the matters of its competence.

E) Prepare an annual report that will be submitted to the Executive, Legislative and Judicial Powers.

6) For the fulfillment of the tasks envisaged in Chapters III and IV of this law, the Board may address, through the intervening judicial body or the representative of the Public Prosecutor's Office, any public office, in order to request the documents and other documents elements necessary for the clarification by the Judge of the facts denounced.

7) In the execution of its functions, the Board will have the permanent legal advice of the Court Prosecutor and Attorney General of the Nation, on formal and procedural aspects (articles 1 and 6 of the Organic Law of the Public Prosecutor and Prosecutor).

8) The Board constitutes a Body with technical independence in the exercise of its functions. Report monthly, by any suitable means, to the Court Prosecutor and Attorney General of the Nation on the activities carried out in relation to the tasks envisaged in the 2nd), 3rd) and 4th) of this article, as well as any resolution adopted about impediments, excuses or challenges that, in the opinion of the Body, any of its members may have regarding the matters to be considered by it. Notwithstanding the provisions of paragraph 7) above, the Office of the Prosecutor of the Court and the Attorney General of the Nation may provide the Advisory Board with administrative and accounting support for the best fulfillment of its tasks that it will request.

Text given by law 17,296 of February 21, 2001.

Substituted text: "The Board constitutes a body with technical independence in the exercise of its functions. It will act under the superintendence of the Court Prosecutor and Attorney General of the Nation."

Source: http://www.oas.org/juridico/spanish/legis_recursos_pub.htm. Acessed in November 2, 2018.

VENEZUELA	*ORGANIC LAW OF THE PUBLIC ADMINISTRATION THE NATIONAL ASSEMBLY OF THE BOLIVARIAN REPUBLIC OF VENEZUELA DECREE* *The next,* *ORGANIC LAW OF THE PUBLIC ADMINISTRATION* *TITLE I* *GENERAL DISPOSITION* *Object of the Law* *Article 1*

The purpose of this Law is to establish the principles and bases that govern the organization and operation of the Public Administration; the principles and guidelines of the organization and operation of the National Public Administration and functionally decentralized administration; as well as regulating management commitments; create mechanisms to promote participation and control over public policies and outcomes; and establish the basic rules on public records and archives.

Area of application

Article 2

The provisions of this Law shall be applicable to the National Public Administration. The principles and norms that refer in general to the Public Administration, or expressly to the states, metropolitan districts and municipalities will be of obligatory observance by these, who will have to develop them within the scope of their respective competences.

The provisions of this Law may be supplementary to the other organs of the Public Power.

TITLE II

PRINCIPLES AND BASES OF THE FUNCTIONING AND ORGANIZATION OF THE PUBLIC ADMINISTRATION

Main Objective of the Public Administration

Article 3

The Public Administration shall have as main objective of its organization and functioning to give effectiveness to the principles, values and norms enshrined in the Constitution of the Bolivarian Republic of Venezuela and, in particular, to guarantee all persons, in accordance with the principle of progressivity and without discrimination some, the enjoyment and inalienable, indivisible and interdependent exercise of human rights.

Principle of Legality

Article 4

The Public Administration is organized and acts in accordance with the principle of legality, by which the assignment, distribution and exercise of its powers is subject to the Constitution of the Bolivarian Republic of Venezuela, to laws and administrative acts of a normative nature, dictated formally and previously in accordance with the law, in guarantee and protection of public liberties that enshrines the democratic regime to individuals.

Principle of Public Administration at the Service of Individuals

Article 5

The Public Administration is at the service of individuals and in its performance will give preference to the attention of the population's requirements and the satisfaction of their needs.

The Public Administration must assure individuals the effectiveness of their rights when they relate to it. It will also have among its objectives the continuous improvement of procedures, services and public services, in accordance with the established policies and taking into account the available resources, determining in this regard the services provided by the Public Administration services, its contents and the corresponding quality standards.

Guarantees that Public Administration Should Offer to Individuals

Article 6

The Public Administration will develop its activity and will be organized so that individuals:

1. They can resolve their issues, be assisted in the formal drafting of administrative documents, and receive information of general interest by telephone, computer and telematic means.

2. They can present claims without the character of administrative resources, on the operation of the Public Administration.

3. They can easily access up-to-date information on the organizational structure of the bodies and entities of the Public Administration, as well as informative guides on the administrative procedures, services and benefits they offer.

Source:
http://www.ventanalegal.com/leyes/
ley_organica_administracion_publica.html. Acessed in November 2, 2018.

1 http://www.anticorrupcion.gov.ar/documentos/recupero%20de%20 activos%20-%20 form%20red.pdf. acesso em 23.09.11

It is the duty of public officials to do what the law determines. If legal provision is lacking for the practice of administrative acts, then they should not be practiced, as is the linkage of agent's conduct to law in the rule of law.

These norms are also modified to suit the temper of each elected government. That's why the ethical and moral principles inserted in each one of them, most of time, are no more than dead words.

CHAPTER 9

Symmetries of the Extraterritorial Crimes against the Public Administrations of Mercosur

Baruch de Spinoza (2002: 45, 348) says with propriety that "every separate effect of the Cause is a Nothing that seems to be Something" and goes on to say that "this occurs because of two goods, we will look under the direction of Reason, the greater, and, of two evils, the lesser".

The crime has become globalized. Corruption with money and public revenues occurs in one country and the product is washed in another, in a fraction of the time.

This is why the principle of extraterritoriality of crimes founded on universal or cosmopolitan justice needs to be better considered.

Professor Mireille Delmas-Marty (2003: 13), when addressing the Law Market and Corruption, is manifested by the necessary worldwide reciprocity on the principle of extraterritoriality, as follows:

"In certain sectors, such as that of international corruption, extraterritoriality may prove unfavorable to domestic firms. a well-known example is that of the American law against the practice of acts of corruption abroad, adopted in 1977, shortly after the scandals of the seventies (and, in particular, the Lockeed case) of extraterritorial application, so as to punish acts of corruption committed abroad by US companies or their affiliated companies, this text is, however, in accordance with international law, since such practices result in anti-competitive effects on the US. But with the risk of weakening American companies in the face of their competitors, so that other countries have not adopted similar legislation."In this comparative analysis of territoriality and extraterritoriality of crimes and acts of improbity with public funds that go beyond the borders of the victimized country, we begin by noting that all Mercosur countries adopt the Criminal Principle of territoriality in their criminal codes, as the framework of symmetries we elaborate:

9.1 - Table on symmetries of the principle of territoriality in Mercosur Criminal Law

ARGENTINA	APPLICATION OF THE CRIMINAL LAW ARTICLE 1.- THIS CODE WILL APPLY: 1°.- For crimes committed or whose effects must occur in the territory of the Argentine Nation, or in the places subject to its jurisdiction; 2°.- For crimes committed abroad by agents or employees of Argentine authorities in the performance of their position.
BRAZIL	Art. 5th - Brazilian law, without prejudice to conventions, treaties and rules of international law, applies to crime committed in the national territory. (wording given by Law No. 7.209 of 1984)
PARAGUAY	Article 6.- events carried out in the national territory 1°. The Paraguayan criminal law will apply to all the facts punishable offenses carried out in the national territory or on board Paraguayan ships or aircraft.
URUGUAY	9. (Criminal law and territory) The crimes committed in the territory of the republic, will be punished according to Uruguayan law, be they national or foreign authors, without prejudice to the exceptions established by domestic public law or by international law.

VENEZUELA	CÓDIGO ORGÁNICO PROCESAL PENAL Decreto N° 9.042 12 de junio de 2012 HUGO CHAVEZ FRIAS Presidente de la República Chapter II Of the Competition for the Territory Territorial Competition
	Article 58. The territorial jurisdiction of the courts is determined by the place where the crime or lack has been consummated.
	In case of imperfect offense, the one in the place where the last act directed to the commission of the crime has been executed shall be competent.
	In cases of continuing or permanent crime, the knowledge shall correspond to the court of the place where continuity or permanence has ceased or the last known act of the crime has been committed.
	In cases of crime or imperfect offense committed in part within the national territory, the court of the place where the action or omission has been carried out totally or partially or the result has been verified shall be competent. Subsidiary competences
	Article 59. When the place of the consummation of the crime, or that of the performance of the last act directed to its commission, or that where continuity or permanence has ceased, the knowledge of the cause shall correspond, according to its order, to the court :
	1. That he exercises jurisdiction in the place where there are elements that serve for the investigation of the act and the identification of the author.
	2. Of the residence of the first researched or investigated.
	3. That you receive the first request of the Public Ministry for research purposes.

Exterritoriality

Article 60. In cases of crimes committed outside the territory of the Republic, when the process can or should be followed in Venezuela, it will be competent, if there is no court expressly designated by special law, to exercise jurisdiction in the place where it is located. the last residence of the accused or imputed; and, if he or she has not resided in the Republic, the jurisdiction of the place where he arrives or is at the moment of requesting the prosecution will be competent.

The principles of the application of the criminal law in time and space are adopted symmetrically within the Mercosur member countries and are as follows:

1– territoriality;
2– nationality;
3– defense, guardianship or protection;
4– representation or flag; and
5– nationality.

We will not comment further on each of the principles because it is not the focus of this work.

We note, however, that Brazil also adopts the principle of extraterritoriality, as foreseen in art. 7 of its Penal Code:

"Extraterritoriality (Law No. 7,209 of 1984)

Art. 7th - They are subject to Brazilian law, although committed abroad:

I - crimes:

a) against the life or liberty of the President of the Republic;

b) against the patrimony or public faith of the union, Federal District, state, territory, municipality, public company, mixed economy society, autarky or foundation instituted by the Public Power;

c) against the public administration, by who is in its service;

d) of genocide, when the agent is Brazilian or domiciled in Brazil;

II - crimes:

a) that, by treaty or convention, Brazil undertook to repay;

b) practiced by Brazilian;

c) practiced on Brazilian aircraft, vessels, or on private property, when in foreign territory and where they are not tried there.

§ 1° - In the cases of item I, the agent is punished according to Brazilian law, even if acquitted or convicted abroad.

§ 2° - In the cases of item II, the application of Brazilian law depends on the following conditions:

a) enter the agent in the national territory;

b) be punishable also in the country where it was practiced;

c) there is the crime included among those for which the Brazilian law authorizes extradition;

d) the person not acquitted abroad or has not served his sentence;

e) the offender was not pardoned abroad or, for other reasons, punishability was not extinguished under the most favorable law.

§ 3° - The Brazilian law also applies to the crime committed by a foreigner against Brazilians outside

Brazil, if, subject to the conditions set forth in the previous paragraph:

a) no extradition was requested or refused;

b) there was a request from the Minister of Justice."

In item "i" letter "c", the active subject of the crime or act of corruption is that which is in the service of the Public Administration. See that even when the crime is committed abroad, the active subject will be punished by brazilian law, by application of the principle of extraterritoriality.

However, the combination of this principle with the rites required by national and international procedural laws, makes the prosecution of the criminal and the application of the punishment are prolonged over time, leading, in some cases, to the extinguish the right of the state to punish and almost always to the impunity of the criminals and, consequently to the descredit of the Judiciary Branch.

There is lack of uniformity of criminal, procedural and administrative disciplinary legislation in Mercosur. I believe the uniformity would be very useful for all economic blocs, including the the creation of a specialized administrative justice, as it exists in I Italy has done, point we discuss in Book 5 of this encyclopedia.

By all we have shown it is clear that Mercosur member countries are governed symmetrically by principles that fight crimes inside and outside their territory.

Next and with straight inspiration of the international law, by some tables that we have ellaborated, I believe it posible to show clearly the symmetry between crimes against Mercosur Public Administrations.

9.2 - Table of symmetries in extraterritorial crimes against the Mercosur Public Administrations - MPA

ARGENTINA	TITLE XI
PENAL CODE OF ARGENTINA **LEY 11.179 (T.O. 1984 actualizado)**	CRIMES AGAINST PUBLIC ADMINISTRATION (...) Chapter VI Bribery and influence peddling (Title of the chapter replaced by Article 30 of Law No. 25.188 B.O. 1/11/1999. Validity: eight days after its publication.) ARTICLE 256. - Will be repressed with imprisonment or imprisonment from one to six years and perpetual special disqualification, the public official who by himself or by interposed person, receives money or any other gift or accepts a direct or indirect promise, to make, delay or stop doing something relative to their functions (Article replaced by Article 31 of Law N ° 25.188 B.O. 1/11/1999. Validity: eight days after its publication.) ARTICLE 256 bis - Will be punished with imprisonment or imprisonment from one to six years and perpetual special disqualification to exercise public office, which by itself or by interposed request or receive money or any other gift or accept a direct or indirect promise, to to make undue use of his influence before a public official, so that he may do, delay or stop doing something related to his functions.

If that conduct was intended to improperly assert an influence before a magistrate of the Judiciary or the Public Ministry, in order to obtain the issuance, issuance, delay or omission of an opinion, resolution or ruling on matters submitted to its jurisdiction, the maximum The penalty of imprisonment or imprisonment will be increased to twelve years.

(Article incorporated by Article 32 of Law N ° 25.188 B.O. 1/11/1999. Validity: eight days after its publication.)

ARTICLE 257. - Will be repressed with imprisonment or imprisonment of four to twelve years and perpetual special disqualification, the magistrate of the Judicial Power or the Public Prosecutor who, by himself or through an interposed person, receives money or any other gift or accepts a direct or indirect promise to issue, dictate, delay or omit to dictate a resolution, ruling or opinion, in matters submitted to its competence

(Article replaced by article 33 of Law N ° 25,188 B.O. 1/11/1999. Validity: eight days after its publication.)

ARTICLE 258. - He shall be punished with imprisonment from one to six years, who directly or indirectly gives or offers gifts in pursuit of any of the conducts repressed by articles 256 and 256 bis, first paragraph. If the gift is made or offered for the purpose of obtaining any of the conducts typified in articles 256 bis, second paragraph and 257, the penalty shall be imprisonment or imprisonment of two to six years. If the guilty party is a public official, he will also suffer special disqualification from two to six years in the first case and from three to ten years in the second.

(Article replaced by Article 34 of Law N ° 25.188 B.O. 1/11/1999. Validity: eight days after its publication.)

ARTICLE 258 bis - A prison sentence of one (1) to six (6) years and a perpetual special disqualification to perform the public function shall be punished, whether directly or indirectly offered, promised or unduly granted to a public official of another State. or of an international public organization, either for their benefit or a third party, sums of money or any other object of pecuniary value or other compensation such as gifts, favors, promises or advantages, in exchange for said official performing or omitting to perform an act related to the exercise of their public functions, or to assert the influence derived from their position in a matter related to a transaction of an economic, financial or commercial nature.

A public official of another State, or of any territorial entity recognized by the Argentine Nation, shall be understood as any person who has been designated or elected to perform a public function, in any of its levels or territorial divisions of government, or in any class of an organism, agency or public company in which said State exerts a direct or indirect influence.

(Article replaced by Article 30 of Law N ° 27.401 B.O. 1/12/2017 Effective: ninety (90) days after its publication in the Official Gazette of the Argentine Republic)

(ARTICLE 259. - He shall be punished with imprisonment from one month to two years and absolute disqualification from one to six years, the public official who admits gifts, which were delivered in consideration of his office, while he remains in the exercise of the office. The one who presents or offers the gift will be repressed with imprisonment of one month to one year.

ARTICLE 259 bis - With respect to the offenses set forth in this Chapter, a fine of two (2) to five (5) times the amount or value of the money, gift, undue benefit or pecuniary advantage offered or delivered shall be imposed jointly.

(Article incorporated by Article 31 of Law No. 27.401 B.O. 1/12/2017 Effective: ninety (90) days after its publication in the Official Gazette of the Argentine Republic)

Chapter VII
Embezzlement of public funds

ARTICLE 260. - The public official who gives to the funds or effects that will administer an application different from the one to which they were destined will be repressed with special disqualification from one month to three years. If it results in damage or obstruction of the service to which they were intended, the guilty party shall also be liable to a fine of twenty to fifty percent of the amount distracted.

ARTICLE 261. - It will be repressed with imprisonment or imprisonment of two to ten years and absolute permanent disqualification, the public official that sustratosre flows or effects whose administration, perception or custody has been entrusted to him by reason of his position. It will be repressed with the same penalty the official who will use for his own benefit or for a third party, jobs or services paid by a public administration.

ARTICLE 262. - It will be repressed with a fine of twenty to sixty percent of the value subtracted, the public official who, due to negligence or due to non-observance of the regulations or duties of his office, gives occasion to be carried out by another person the subtraction of flows or effects discussed in the previous article.

ARTICLE 263. - Those who administrate or guard assets belonging to establishments of public instruction or charity, as well as administrators and depositaries of seized, seized or deposited funds by competent authority, although belonging to individuals, are subject to the above provisions.

ARTICLE 264. - The public official who, having expedited funds, unjustifiably delays an ordinary payment or decreed by a competent authority will be repressed with special disqualification for one to six months. In the same penalty, the public official who, requested by the competent authority, will refuse to deliver a quantity or effect deposited or placed under its custody or administration.

Chapter VIII
Negotiations incompatible with the exercise of public functions

ARTICLE 265. - Will be repressed with imprisonment or imprisonment of one (1) to six (6) years and perpetual special disqualification, the public official who, directly, by interposed person or by simulated act, is interested in view of his own benefit or of a third party, in any contract or operation in which it intervenes due to its position.

A fine of two (2) to five (5) times of the value of the improper benefit sought or obtained shall also be applied.

This provision shall be applicable to the arbitrators, amicable conciliators, experts, accountants, tutors, curators, executors, trustees and liquidators, with respect to the functions fulfilled in the character of such.

(Article replaced by Article 32 of Law N ° 27.401 B.O. 1/12/2017 Effective: ninety (90) days after its publication in the Official Gazette of the Argentine Republic)

Chapter IX
Illegal exactions

ARTICLE 266. - The public official shall be punished with imprisonment of one (1) to four (4) years and special disqualification of one (1) to (5) five years, abusing his position, requesting, demanding or having to pay or improperly deliver, by itself or through an interposed person, a contribution, a right or a gift or collect higher rights than those that correspond.

A fine of two (2) to five (5) times the amount of the levy will also be applied.

(Article replaced by article 33 of Law N ° 27.401 B.O. 1/12/2017 Effective: ninety (90) days after its publication in the Official Gazette of the Argentine Republic)

ARTICLE 267. - If intimidation is employed or superior order, commission, injunction or other legitimate authorization is invoked, the prison may be increased up to four years and the disqualification may be up to six years.

ARTICLE 268. - It will be repressed with imprisonment of two (2) to six (6) years and absolute perpetual disqualification, the public official who converts the exactions expressed in the previous articles to his own or third party's benefit.

A fine of two (2) to five (5) times the amount of the levy will also be applied.

(Article replaced by Article 34 of Law No. 27.401 B.O. 1/12/2017 Effective: ninety (90) days after its publication in the Official Gazette of the Argentine Republic)

Chapter VII
Embezzlement of public funds

ARTICLE 260. - The public official who gives to the funds or effects that will administer an application different from the one to which they were destined will be repressed with special disqualification from one month to three years. If it results in damage or obstruction of the service to which they were intended, the guilty party shall also be liable to a fine of twenty to fifty percent of the amount distracted.

ARTICLE 261. - It will be repressed with imprisonment or imprisonment of two to ten years and absolute permanent disqualification, the public official that sustratosre flows or effects whose administration, perception or custody has been entrusted to him by reason of his position. It will be repressed with the same penalty the official who will use for his own benefit or for a third party, jobs or services paid by a public administration.

ARTICLE 262. - It will be repressed with a fine of twenty to sixty percent of the value subtracted, the public official who, due to negligence or due to non-observance of the regulations or duties of his office, gives occasion to be carried out by another person the subtraction of flows or effects discussed in the previous article.

ARTICLE 263. - Those who administrate or guard assets belonging to establishments of public instruction or charity, as well as administrators and depositaries of seized, seized or deposited funds by competent authority, although belonging to individuals, are subject to the above provisions.

ARTICLE 264. - The public official who, having expedited funds, unjustifiably delays an ordinary payment or decreed by a competent authority will be repressed with special disqualification for one to six months. In the same penalty, the public official who, requested by the competent authority, will refuse to deliver a quantity or effect deposited or placed under its custody or administration.

Chapter VIII
Negotiations incompatible with the exercise of public functions

ARTICLE 265. - Will be repressed with imprisonment or imprisonment of one (1) to six (6) years and perpetual special disqualification, the public official who, directly, by interposed person or by simulated act, is interested in view of his own benefit or of a third party, in any contract or operation in which it intervenes due to its position.

A fine of two (2) to five (5) times of the value of the improper benefit sought or obtained shall also be applied.

This provision shall be applicable to the arbitrators, amicable conciliators, experts, accountants, tutors, curators, executors, trustees and liquidators, with respect to the functions fulfilled in the character of such.

(Article replaced by Article 32 of Law N ° 27.401 B.O. 1/12/2017 Effective: ninety (90) days after its publication in the Official Gazette of the Argentine Republic)

Chapter IX
Illegal exactions

ARTICLE 266. - The public official shall be punished with imprisonment of one (1) to four (4) years and special disqualification of one (1) to (5) five years, abusing his position, requesting, demanding or having to pay or improperly deliver, by itself or through an interposed person, a contribution, a right or a gift or collect higher rights than those that correspond.

A fine of two (2) to five (5) times the amount of the levy will also be applied.

(Article replaced by article 33 of Law N ° 27.401 B.O. 1/12/2017 Effective: ninety (90) days after its publication in the Official Gazette of the Argentine Republic)

ARTICLE 267. - If intimidation is employed or superior order, commission, injunction or other legitimate authorization is invoked, the prison may be increased up to four years and the disqualification may be up to six years.

ARTICLE 268. - It will be repressed with imprisonment of two (2) to six (6) years and absolute perpetual disqualification, the public official who converts the exactions expressed in the previous articles to his own or third party's benefit.

A fine of two (2) to five (5) times the amount of the levy will also be applied.

(Article replaced by Article 34 of Law No. 27.401 B.O. 1/12/2017 Effective: ninety (90) days after its publication in the Official Gazette of the Argentine Republic)

Chapter IX bis
Illicit enrichment of officials and employees

ARTICLE 268 (1). - It will be repressed with the penalty of article 256, the public official who for profit purposes will use for himself or for a third party information or data of a reserved nature of which he has become aware by reason of his position.

A fine of two (2) to five (5) times of the profit obtained will also be applied. (Paragraph incorporated by Article 35 of Law No. 27.401 B.O. 1/12/2017 Effective: ninety (90) days after its publication in the Official Gazette of the Argentine Republic)

ARTICLE 268 (2) - Shall be punished with imprisonment from two (2) to six (6) years, a fine of two (2) to five (5) times the value of the enrichment, and permanent absolute disqualification, which upon being duly required , I will not justify the origin of an appreciable patrimonial enrichment of yours or of a person interposed to disguise it, occurring after the assumption of a position or public employment and up to two (2) years after having ceased to perform. (Paragraph substituted by Article 36 of Law N ° 27.401 B.O. 1/12/2017 Effective: ninety (90) days after its publication in the Official Gazette of the Argentine Republic)

It will be understood that there was enrichment not only when the patrimony had been increased with money, things or goods, but also when debts had been canceled or extinguished obligations that affected it.

The person interposed to disguise the enrichment will be repressed with the same penalty as the perpetrator.

(Article replaced by article 38 of Law N ° 25.188 B.O. 1/11/1999. Validity: eight days after its publication.)

ARTICLE 268 (3) - A prison sentence of fifteen days to two years and a perpetual special disqualification shall be punished by the fact that, by virtue of his office, he is required by law to submit an affidavit of equity and maliciously omits to do so.

The offense will be set when, upon reliable notification of the respective summons, the obligated party has not complied with the aforementioned duties within the deadlines set by the law whose application corresponds.

In the same penalty shall incur the maliciously, falsely or omit to insert the data that the said sworn statements must contain in accordance with applicable laws and regulations.

(Article incorporated by article 39 of Law N° 25,188 B.O. 1/11/1999. Validity: eight days after its publication.)

Chapter X
Prevarication

ARTICLE 269. - A fine of three thousand pesos to seventy-five thousand pesos and perpetual absolute disqualification will be imposed by the judge who will dictate resolutions contrary to the express law invoked by the parties or by the same or cited, to found them, false facts or resolutions.

If the sentence is condemnatory in criminal case, the penalty will be three to fifteen years of imprisonment or prison and permanent absolute disqualification.

The provisions of the first paragraph of this article shall apply, where appropriate, to friendly arbitrators and arbitrators.

(Note Infoleg: fine updated by Article 1 of Law N° 24.286 B.O. 29/12/1993)

ARTICLE 270. - A fine of two thousand five hundred to thirty thousand pesos and absolute disqualification from one to six years shall be punished with a fine that shall be ordered by a judge who decrees preventive detention for an offense under which it does not proceed or prolongs the preventive detention which, computed in the form established in article 24, has exhausted the maximum penalty that could correspond to the defendant for the imputed crime.

(Note Infoleg: fine updated by Article 1 of Law N° 24.286 B.O. 29/12/1993)

ARTICLE 271. - It will be repressed with a fine of two thousand five hundred to thirty thousand pesos, and special disqualification of one to six years, the lawyer or judicial agent who defends or represents opposing parties in the same trial, simultaneously or successively or that of any otherwise, it will deliberately harm the cause entrusted to it.

(Note Infoleg: fine updated by Article 1 of Law N° 24.286 B.O. 29/12/1993)

ARTICLE 272. - The provision of the previous article will be applicable to the prosecutors, advisers and other officials in charge of issuing their opinion before the authorities.

BRAZIL **PENAL CODE** **Decreto-lei nº 1.848 7 1940**	TITLE XI OF THE CRIMES AGAINST THE PUBLIC ADMINISTRATION

TITLE XI
OF THE CRIMES AGAINST THE PUBLIC
ADMINISTRATION

CHAPTER I
OF THE CRIMES PRACTICED
BY PUBLIC OFFICIAL
AGAINST THE ADMINISTRATION IN GENERAL

peculation

Art. 312 - To approve the public official of money, value or any other mobile, public or private property, of which he has possession by reason of the charge, or to divert it, for his own benefit or that of others:

Penalty - imprisonment, from two to twelve years, and fine.

§ 1 - The same penalty is applied if the public official, even if he does not have the possession of the money, value or good, subtracts it, or attends to it being stolen, for his own benefit or that of others, using the facility provided by the quality of employee.

Peculate guilty

§ 2nd - If the official is guilty of the crime of another:

Penalty - detention, from three months to a year.

§ 3 - In the case of the previous paragraph, the repair of the damage, if it precedes the irrefutable sentence, extinguishes the punishability; if it is later, reduce the penalty imposed by half.

Peculato by mistake of another

Art. 313 - Take advantage of money or any utility that, in the exercise of the position, received by mistake of another:

Penalty - imprisonment, from one to four years, and fine.

Irregular use of funds or public revenues

Art. 315 - Give the funds or public income application different from that established in law:

Penalty - detention, from one to three months, or fine.

concussion

Art. 316 - To demand, for himself or for another, directly or indirectly, even if outside the function or before assuming it, but because of it, undue advantage:

Penalty - imprisonment, from two to eight years, and fine.

Excess of exaction

§ 1 - If the official demands tribute or social contribution that he knows or should know improperly, or, when due, he uses in the collection a degrading or burdensome means, which the law does not authorize: (Drafting given by Law n° 8.137, of 27.12. 1990)

Penalty - imprisonment, from 3 (three) to 8 (eight) years, and fine. (Drafting given by Law No. 8.137, of 27.12.1990)

§ 2nd - If the official deviates, for his own benefit or that of another, what he received improperly to collect the public coffers:

Penalty - imprisonment, from two to twelve years, and fine.

Passive corruption

Art. 317 - Request or receive, for himself or for another, directly or indirectly, although outside the function or before assuming it, but due to it, undue advantage, or accepting a promise of such advantage:

Penalty - imprisonment, from 2 (two) to 12 (twelve) years, and fine. (Drafting given by Law No. 10.763, of 12.11.2003)

§ 1 - The penalty is increased by one third, if, as a consequence of the advantage or promise, the official delays or fails to practice any act of office or practices it infringing functional duty.

§ 2 - If the official practices, he stops practicing or delaying an act of his own accord, with a breach of a functional duty, giving in at the request or influence of another:

Penalty - detention, from three months to one year, or fine.

Facilitation of contraband or mishandling

Art. 318 - Facilitate, with a breach of functional duty, the practice of contraband or misdirection (article 334):

Penalty - imprisonment, from 3 (three) to 8 (eight) years, and fine. (Drafting given by Law No. 8.137, of 27.12.1990)

Prevarication

Art. 319 - To delay or to stop practicing, improperly, act of office, or to practice it against express disposition of law, to satisfy interest or personal feeling:

Penalty - detention, from three months to a year, and a fine.

Art. 319-A. Leave the Director of Penitentiary and / or public agent, to fulfill his duty to ban the prisoner access to telephone, radio or similar device, which allows communication with other prisoners or with the external environment: (Included by Law No. 11,466 , 2007).

▢

4266/5000
Influence Traffic (Drafting given by Law n° 9.127, of 1995)

Article 332 - Request, demand, collect or obtain, for himself or for another, advantage or promise of advantage, under the pretext of influencing an act performed by a public official in the exercise of the function: (Drafting given by Law No. 9.127 , 1995)

Penalty - imprisonment, from 2 (two) to 5 (five) years, and fine. (Drafting given by Law No. 9.127, of 1995)

Single Paragraph - The penalty is increased by half, if the agent alleges or implies that the advantage is also intended for the official. (Drafting given by Law No. 9.127, of 1995)

Active corruption

Art. 333 - Offering or promising undue advantage to a public official, in order to determine it to practice, omit or delay an act of office:

Penalty - imprisonment, from 2 (two) to 12 (twelve) years, and fine. (Drafting given by Law No. 10.763, of 12.11.2003)

Sole Paragraph - The penalty is increased by one third, if, due to the advantage or promise, the employee delays or omits act of office, or practices it infringing functional duty.

embezzlement

Art. 334. Iludir, in whole or in part, the payment of duty or tax due for the entry, exit or consumption of merchandise (Drafting given by Law No. 13,008 of 26.6.2014)

Penalty - imprisonment, from 1 (one) to 4 (four) years. (Drafting given by Law n° 13.008, of 26.6.2014)

§ 1o Enter in the same penalty who: (Drafting given by Law n° 13.008, of 26.6.2014)

II - practice made assimilated, in special law, the descamination; (Drafting given by Law n° 13.008, of 26.6.2014)

- III - sells, exhibits for sale, keeps in deposit or, in any way, uses for its own or another's benefit, in the exercise of commercial or industrial activity, merchandise of foreign origin that was smuggled into the country or fraudulently imported or that it can be a product of clandestine introduction into the national territory or of fraudulent importation by another; (Drafting given by Law n° 13.008, of 26.6.2014)

IV - acquires, receives or conceals, for personal gain or for others, in the exercise of commercial or industrial activity, goods of foreign origin, unattended legal documentation or accompanied by documents that are known to be false. (Drafting given by Law n° 13.008, of 26.6.2014)

§ 2o For commercial purposes, for the purposes of this article, any form of irregular or clandestine trade in foreign merchandise, including that exercised in residences, has been assigned. (Drafting given by Law n° 13.008, of 26.6.2014)

§ 3° The penalty is applied in double if the crime of misguidance is practiced in air, maritime or fluvial transport. (Drafting given by Law n° 13.008, of 26.6.2014)

smuggling

Art. 334-A. Import or export prohibited merchandise: (Included by Law n° 13.008, of 26.6.2014)

Penalty - seclusion, from 2 (two) to 5 (five) years. (Included by Law n° 13.008, of 26.6.2014)

§ 1o Affix in the same penalty who: (Included by Law n° 13.008, of 26.6.2014)

I - practice made assimilated, in special law, to contraband; (Included by Law n° 13.008, of 26.6.2014)

II - imports or exports clandestinely merchandise that depends on the registration, analysis or authorization of the competent public body; (Included by Law n° 13.008, of 26.6.2014)

III - reinseer Brazilian merchandise destined for export in the national territory;(Included by Law n° 13.008, of 26.6.2014)

- IV - sells, exposes for sale, keeps in deposit or, in any way, uses for own or another's benefit, in the exercise of commercial or industrial activity, merchandise prohibited by Brazilian law; (Included by Law n° 13.008, of 26.6.2014)

V - acquires, receives or conceals, for its own benefit or that of others, in the exercise of commercial or industrial activity, merchandise prohibited by Brazilian law. § 2 - Commercial activities, for the purposes of this article, are equated to any form of irregular or clandestine trade in foreign merchandise, including that exercised in residences. (Included by Law n° 4.729, of 14.7.1965)

PARAGUAY **PENAL CODE OF PARAGUAY** **LAW NO. 1.160 / 97**	TITLE XI OF THE CRIMES AGAINST THE PUBLIC ADMINISTRATION CHAPTER I OF THE CRIMES PRACTICED BY PUBLIC OFFICIAL AGAINST THE ADMINISTRATION IN GENERAL CHAPTER III PUNITIVE FACTS AGAINST THE EXERCISE OF PUBLIC FUNCTIONS Article 300.- Passive bribery 1° The official who requests, will be allowed to promise or accept a benefit in exchange for a consideration derived from a behavior characteristic of the service that he has performed or will perform in the future, will be punished with imprisonment of up to three years or with a fine.

2º The judge or arbitrator who requested, will be allowed to promise or accept a benefit such as consideration of a resolution or other judicial activity that has been carried out or that In the future, he will be punished with imprisonment of up to five years or a fine.

3º In these cases, the attempt will also be punished.

Article 301.- Aggravated passive bribery

1º The official who requests, will be allowed to promise or accept a benefit in exchange for an act of service already performed or will be carried out in the future, and that will harm his duties, will be punished with imprisonment of up to five years.

2º The judge or arbitrator who requested, will be allowed to promise or accept a benefit in exchange for a resolution or other judicial activity already carried out or that will be carried out in the future, and injures his judicial duties, will be punished with imprisonment of up to ten years .

3º In these cases, the attempt will also be punished.

In the cases of the preceding paragraphs, the provisions of article 57 shall also apply.

Article 302.- Bribery

1º Anyone who offers, promises or guarantees a benefit to an official in exchange for an act of service already performed or to be performed in the future, and which depends on his discretion, will be punished with imprisonment of up to two years or with penalty fee.

2º Anyone who offers, promises or guarantees a benefit to a judge or arbitrator in exchange for a resolution or other judicial activity already carried out or that will be carried out in the future, will be punished by imprisonment of up to three years or a fine.

Article 303.- Aggravated bribery

1° Anyone who offers, promises or guarantees a benefit to an official in exchange for an act of service already performed or to be carried out in the future, and which damages his duties, shall be punished with imprisonment of up to three years.

2. Anyone who offers, promises or guarantees to a judge or arbitrator a benefit in exchange for a resolution or other judicial activity, already carried out or that will be carried out in the future, and which injures his judicial duties, will be punished with imprisonment of one to five years

3° In these cases, the attempt will also be punished.

Article 304.- Additional provisions

1° It will be equated to the performance of an act of service, in the sense of the articles of this chapter, the omission of the same.

2° It will be considered as a benefit of an arbitrator, within the meaning of the articles of this chapter, the remuneration that the latter will request, be promised or accepted by one party, without the knowledge of the other, or if a party offers it to them, , without knowledge of the other.

Article 305.- Prevarication

1° The judge, arbitrator or other official who, having in charge of the direction or decision of a legal matter, decides violating the right to favor or harm one of the parties, will be punished by imprisonment for two to five years .

2° In particularly serious cases, the penalty of deprivation of liberty may be increased up to ten years.

URUGUAY	TITLE IV
PENAL CODE	CRIMES AGAINST PUBLIC ADMINISTRATION
	CHAPTER I

Art. 153. Peculado. The public official who appropriated the money or personal property, that is in possession by reason of his office, belonging to the State, or individuals, for their own benefit or that of others, will be punished with one year of imprisonment to six years of penitentiary and with special disqualification from two to six years.

Art. 154. Mitigating circumstance. It constitutes a special attenuating circumstance, the fact of dealing with money or things of little value and the repair of the damage previously to the fiscal accusation.

Art. 155. Peculation for taking advantage of another's error. The public official who, in exercise of his position, taking advantage of the error of another, receives or withholds, unduly, for his own benefit or for others, money or other movable property, will be punished with three to eighteen months of prison and two to four years of disqualification special.

Art. 156. Concussion. The public official who, with abuse of his status as such or the office he performs, compels or induces someone to give or unduly promise him or a third party, money or any other benefit, will be punished with twelve months of imprisonment to six years of penitentiary, fine of 50 UR (fifty readjustable units) to 10,000 UR (ten thousand readjustable units) and disqualification from two to six years. The mitigation of article 154. applies to this offense. (35c)

Art. 157. Simple bridging. The public official who, by executing an act of his employment, receives by the same, or by a third party for himself or for a third party, a payment that was not due, or accept the promise of it, will be punished with a penalty of three months of imprisonment to three years of penitentiary, with a fine of 10 UR (ten readjustable units) a

5,000 UR (five thousand readjustable units) and special disqualification from two to four years. The penalty shall be reduced from one third to one half, when the public official accepts the retribution, for an act already fulfilled, relating to his functions. (36)

Art. 158. Qualified bribery. The public official who, for delaying or issuing an act related to his position or for executing an act contrary to the duties of the same, receives for himself or for another, for himself or for another, money or other benefit, or accepts his

promise, will be punished with twelve months of imprisonment to six years of penitentiary, special disqualification of two to six years, and a fine of 50 UR (fifty adjustable units) to 10,000 UR (ten thousand readjustable units). The penalty shall be increased by one third to one half in the following cases: 1) If the event has the effect of granting public employment, stipends, pensions, honors or the favor or damage of the parties litigant civil or criminal trial. 2) If the event has the effect of concluding a contract in which the division to which the official belongs is involved or it is carried out through an abusive use of the legal procedures that must be applied by the Public Administration in the matter of acquisition of goods and services. (36a)

Art. 158 bis. Influence peddling. He who, invoking real or simulated influences, requests, receives for himself or for another, for himself or for another, economic benefit, or accepts his promise, in order to decisively influence a public official to delay or omit an act of his office, or for executing an act contrary to it, will be punished with three months of imprisonment to four years of penitentiary.

The penalty will be reduced from one third to half when the remuneration is accepted, in order to influence decisively, so that the public official exercises an act inherent to his position. The circumstance that the public official, in relation to whom the influences are invoked, is one of the persons included in articles 10 and 11 of the law on the prevention and fight against corruption, will be considered a special aggravating circumstance. (36b)

Art. 159. Bribery. Any person who induces a public official to commit any of the offenses set forth in articles 157 and 158 shall be punished by the mere act of instigation, with a penalty of half to two thirds of the principal penalty established for them. The following shall be considered special aggravating circumstances: 1) That the accused be a police officer or responsible for the prevention, investigation or repression of illicit activities, provided that the offense was committed as a result of or on the occasion of the exercise of his functions, or because of his or her such and that this last circumstance is ostensible for the perpetrator of the crime. 2) That the accused is one of the persons included in articles 10 and 11 of the law on the prevention and fight against corruption. (36c)

VENEZUELA PENAL CODE	TITLE III
	Of crimes against public property
	CHAPTER I From the embezzlement
	Article 195.- Every public official who removes the money or other movable objects from whose collection, custody or administration is in charge by virtue of his functions, will be punished with imprisonment of three to ten years.
	If the harm is not serious, or if it is entirely repaired before the guilty party is brought to trial, he will be imprisoned for three to twenty-one months.

CHAPTER II
Of the concussion

Article 196.- Any official who, by abusing his functions, compels any person to give or promise to himself or to a third party any sum of money or other improper gain or gift, shall be punished by imprisonment from eighteen months to five years. If the sum or thing improperly given or promised is of little value, the prison will be for a period of three to twenty-one months.

Article 197.- Any official who, by abusing his or her functions, induces any person to commit any of the acts referred to in the preceding article, shall be punished by imprisonment of two to sixteen months.

If the public official receives what was not due to him, he only takes advantage of the error of the other, the prison will be three to fifteen months.

If the sum or thing improperly given or promised is of little value, the prison, in the first case, will be from one to ten months; and in the second, from fifteen days to six months.

CHAPTER III
From the corruption of officials

Article 198. - Any official who, by his own or another's account, receives for any act of his duties, in money or otherwise, any compensation that is not owed to him or whose promise he accepts, will be punished by imprisonment of one to two months.

Article 199.- Any public official who, by delaying or omitting any act of his functions or making any which is contrary to the duty that they impose, receives, or makes pledged, money or other utility, either by itself or by means of another person, will be punished with imprisonment of three to five years.

The prison will be four to eight years if the act committed has had the effect:

1.- Confer public jobs, subsidies, pensions or honors, or make it agree that the administration to which the official belongs is interested.

2.- Favor or cause any damage or harm to any of the parties in a civil trial, or to the guilty party in a criminal proceeding.

If the act has resulted in a conviction that restricts individual freedom, which exceeds six months, the prison term will be three to ten years.

Article 200. Anyone who, without achieving his object, endeavors to persuade or induce any public official to commit any of the offenses set forth in the preceding articles shall be punished, when the induction is for the purpose of the official incurring the crime provided for in article 198, with a fine of one hundred fifty to one thousand bolivars; and if it is for the purpose of incurring the one indicated by the

Article 201.- Those who manage to corrupt public officials, causing them to commit any of the crimes provided for in this Chapter, will incur the same penalties as the bribed employees.

Article 202. When the bribery mediates in criminal case in favor of the inmate, on the part of his spouse or of an ascendant, descendant or brother, the penalty that should be imposed on the bribee, under all circumstances, will be reduced by two thirds.

Article 203.- In the cases provided in the preceding articles, the money or object given will be confiscated.

Among the crimes that are most symmetrical in the Mercosur member countries, we can highlight:

1– Passive corruption / Cohecho Pasivo
2– Active corruption / Cohecho activo
3– Bribery / Soborno
4– Smuggling
5– Concussion / Concusión

6– Diversion or irregular employment of public funds or income / Desviación de Caudales Públicos u Despilfarro;

7– Influence Traffic / Tráfico de Influencia;

8– Peculation; and

9– White-collar crimes.

There is so much symmetry among the cited crimes that David Baigun (2006: 28) in describing the crime of smuggling in Argentina, for example, seems to have done for Brazil and other members of Mercosur. Here it is:

> "Law 22.415 regulates the provisions concerning crimes related to the export and import of merchandise. Contraband, a basic criminal offense, is defined as "any action or omission that prevents or hinders, through trickery or deception, the proper exercise of the functions that the law accords to the customs service for control over imports and exports ", providing for imprisonment (6 months to 8 years)."

Let us read what the Brazilian Penal Code says about the crime of smuggling and compare what was said about it in Argentina:

> "Art. 334 importing or exporting of goods prohibited or illicit, in whole or in part, the payment of duty or tax due on entry, exit or consumption of goods:
>
> Penalty - imprisonment, from one to four years."

6 http://www.planalto.gov.br/ccivil_03/decreto-Lei/del2848compilado.htm. accessed on 11.01.2012.

A possible order of verification of the symmetry of the smuggling crime for Argentina and Brazil may be:

1– are offenses consisting of a main command and an accessory (the descriptive type of the conduct and the penalty);

2– are crimes formed by objective element (action or omission) and subjective element (guilt);

3– have as active subject the one that imports or exports illegal merchandise;

4– the passive subject of crime (victim) is the administration of justice; and

5– The juridically protected object to be protected in the crime is the administration of justice and public order.

Similar analysis is made for all other crimes listed in Tables 9.2. This means that symmetry makes it possible to unify criminal law as a means of making effective the fight against corruption stemming from such offenses whose effects spread beyond the border.

9.3 - Brazilian law that amends the Criminal Code and promotes the liability of a natural person who commits an act of corruption against foreign public administration

In 2002 the National Congress voted and the President of the Republic sanctioned Law No. 10,467 of June 11, 2002, which amended the Brazilian Penal Code, typifying crimes committed by citizens against the administration foreign public, as you can see from the transcription below:

"CHAPTER II-A

(Included by Law n° 10.467, of 11.6.2002)

OF THE CRIMES PRACTICED BY PARTICULAR AGAINST THE FOREIGN PUBLIC ADMINISTRATION

Active corruption in international commercial transactions

Art. 337-B. Promise, offer or give, directly or indirectly, an undue advantage to a foreign public official, or to the third person, to determine it to practice, omit or delay the act of trade related to the international commercial transaction: (Included by Law No. 10467, of 11.6.2002)

Penalty - imprisonment, from 1 (one) to 8 (eight) years, and a fine. (Included by Law n° 10467, of 11.6.2002)

Sole Paragraph. The penalty is increased by 1/3 (one third), if, by virtue of the advantage or promise, the foreign public official delays or omits the act ex officio, or practices it infringing a functional duty. (Included by Law n° 10467, of 11.6.2002)

Traffic of influence in international commercial transactions (Included by Law n° 10467, of 11.6.2002)

Art. 337-C. Request, demand, collect or obtain, for himself or for another, directly or indirectly, advantage or promise of advantage under the pretext of influencing an act performed by a foreign public official in the exercise of his functions, related to the international commercial transaction: (Included by Law n° 10467, of 11.6.2002)

Penalty - imprisonment, from 2 (two) to 5 (five) years, and fine. (Included by Law n° 10467, of 11.6.2002)

Sole Paragraph. The penalty is increased by half, if the agent alleges or implies that the advantage is also intended for a foreign official. (Included by Law n° 10467, of 11.6.2002)

Foreign public official (Included by Law n° 10467, of 11.6.2002)

Art. 337-D. A foreign public official is considered, for criminal purposes, who, even if temporarily or without remuneration, holds office, employment or public function in state entities or in diplomatic representations of a foreign country. (Included by Law n° 10467, of 11.6.2002)

Sole Paragraph. It is equated to a foreign public official who exercises office, employment or function in companies controlled, directly or indirectly, by the Public Power of a foreign country or in international public organizations. (Included by Law n° 10467, of 11.6.2002)"

Please note that the following crimes have been criminalized:

1– Active corruption in international commercial transactions; and
2– Influence traffic in international commercial transactions.

The infra-constitutional legislator took the opportunity to say that it is considered a foreign public official, for criminal purposes, who, even temporarily or unpaid, holds a position, job or public function in state entities or in diplomatic representations of a foreign country and, final, equated a foreign public official who holds a position, job or function in controlled companies, directly or indirectly by the Public Power of a foreign country or in international public organizations.

9.4 - New Brazilian law that provides for the administrative and civil liability of legal persons for the practice of acts against public administration, national or foreign

On August 1st, 2013, the National Congress decreed and the President of the Brazilian Republic sanctioned Law No. 12.846, which provides for the administrative and civil liability of legal persons for the practice of acts against the public administration, national or foreign, on which we make some notes, hoping that time will improve both the administrative and judicial processes that seek to sanction the active subjects of the civil and administrative infraction.

I personally know that one of the greates concerne of the foreign governments and entrepeneurs is making any business in which a public official from brazilian public or from Mercosur Administration has to intervine or mediate, because just as the spider weaves its web to catch the prey, so does some brazilian and other public servants from Mercosur. And when they know that the business and contracts will be celebrated with governments or foreign companies, then the greed for bribe increases noticeably.

In June, 2015 I was one of the lectrurers invited by Ms. Adey Hailu, Founder of the African Symposium for "Women in Motion Networking Series: African Symposium in collaboration with The NMBC Global Entrepreneurship Center" in New York. By the quantity and quality of the questions, it was easy, at that day, to comprehend the concerns of many abroad entrepeneurs in how to learn to defend themselves from the greed of brazilian public official.

My advise to them is the same I can say today. Learn, at least, a few, of new brazilian laws against corruption. This can build a firewall between you and the corrupt public servant, be it a manager or a politician one.

Follows a new and important law in which I make some comments that can help you a little, if you intend to make business with brazilian public administration:

"LAW No. 12,846, OF AUGUST 1, 2013.

It provides for administrative and civil liability of legal persons for the practice of acts against public administration, national or foreign.

THE PRESIDENT OF THE REPUBLIC I announce that the National Congress decrees and I sanction the following Law:

CHAPTER I

GENERAL DISPOSITION

Art. 1 This Act provides for the objective administrative and civil liability of legal persons for the practice of acts against public administration, national or foreign.

Sole Paragraph. The provisions of this Law apply to business companies and to simple companies, personified or not, regardless of the form of organization or corporate model adopted, as well as any foundation, associations of entities or persons, or foreign companies, that have their headquarters, subsidiary or representation in the Brazilian territory, constituted de facto or de jure, even temporarily.

Art. 2° The juridical persons will be held objectively responsible, in the administrative and civil spheres, for the harmful acts foreseen in this Law practiced in their interest or benefit, exclusive or not.

Art. 3 The responsibility of the juridical person does not exclude the individual responsibility of its leaders or administrators or of any natural person, author, co-author or participant of the illicit act.

§ 1o The legal entity will be held responsible regardless of the individual responsibility of the natural persons mentioned in the caput.

§ 2° The leaders or administrators will only be held responsible for unlawful acts to the extent of their culpability.

Art. 4 The responsibility of the legal entity remains in the hypothesis of contractual alteration, transformation, incorporation, merger or corporate split.

§ 1o In the merger and incorporation hypothesis, the liability of the successor will be restricted to the obligation of payment of fine and integral reparation of the damage caused, up to the limit of the transferred patrimony, not being applicable the other sanctions foreseen in this Law derived from acts and events occurred before the date of the merger or incorporation, except in the case of simulation or evident intention of fraud, duly proven.

§ 2 Controlled, controlled, linked companies or, within the framework of the respective contract, the consortiums will be jointly and severally liable for the practice of the acts provided for in this Act, restricting such liability to the obligation to pay a fine and full compensation for the damage caused.

CHAPTER II

FROM LEGAL ACTS TO THE NATIONAL OR FOREIGN PUBLIC ADMINISTRATION

Art. 5º.- The following constitute acts that are harmful to public administration, national or foreign, for the purposes of this Law, all those practiced by the legal entities mentioned in the single paragraph of art. 1, that attempt against the public national or foreign patrimony, against principles of the public administration or against the international commitments assumed by Brazil, thus defined:

I - promise, offer or give, directly or indirectly, undue advantage to a public agent, or to the third person related to him;

II - verifiably, finance, finance, sponsor or in any way subsidize the practice of unlawful acts provided for in this Act;

III - verifiably, to use as interposed natural or legal person to conceal or disguise their real interests or the identity of the beneficiaries of the acts practiced;

IV - with regard to bids and contracts:

a) frustrate or fraud, through adjustment, combination or any other file, the competitive nature of the public bidding process;

b) prevent, disrupt or fraud the performance of any act of public bidding procedure;

c) set aside or seek to remove the bidder, by means of fraud or offer of advantage of any kind;

d) public bidding fraud or resulting contract;

e) create, in a fraudulent or irregular manner, a legal entity to participate in a public bid or enter into an administrative contract;

f) obtaining undue advantage or benefit, fraudulently, from modifications or extensions of contracts entered into with the public administration, without authorization in law, in the act inviting the public tender or in the respective contractual instruments; or

g) manipulate or fraud the economic-financial balance of contracts entered into with the public administration;

V - hinder the investigation or inspection activity of public bodies, entities or agents, or intervene in their actions, including within the scope of the regulatory agencies and the oversight bodies of the national financial system.

§ 1 ° Foreign public administration is considered to be state organs and entities or diplomatic representations of a foreign country, of any level or sphere of government, as well as legal persons directly or indirectly controlled by the public power of a foreign country.

§ 2o For the purposes of this Law, international public organizations are equated to foreign public administration.

§ 3° For the purposes of this Law, a foreign public agent will be considered as a person who, although temporarily or without remuneration, exercises office, employment or public function in organs, state entities or diplomatic representations of a foreign country, as well as in controlled legal entities, directly or indirectly, by the public power of a foreign country or in international public organizations.

CHAPTER III

OF ADMINISTRATIVE RESPONSIBILITY

Art. 6º In the administrative sphere, the following sanctions will be applied to the juridical persons considered responsible for the harmful acts foreseen in this Law:

I - fine, in the value of 0.1% (one tenth percent) to 20% (twenty percent) of the gross turnover of the last year prior to the establishment of the administrative process, excluding taxes, which will never be inferior to the advantage that is obtained, when its estimation is possible; Y

II - extraordinary publication of the condemnatory decision.

§ 1o The sanctions will be applied based, isolated or cumulatively, according to the peculiarities of the specific case and the severity and nature of the infractions.

§ 2º The application of the sanctions provided for in this article will be preceded by the legal statement prepared by the Public Advocacy or by the legal assistance body, or equivalent, of the public.

§ 3º The application of the sanctions provided for in this article does not exclude, in any hypothesis, the obligation of integral reparation of the damage caused.

§ 4º In the hypothesis of item I of the caput, if it is not possible to use the criterion of the value of the gross billing of the legal entity, the fine will be R $ 6,000.00 (six thousand reais) to R $ 60,000,000, 00 (sixty) million reais).

§ 5o The extraordinary publication of the condemnatory decision will take place in the form of an extract of judgment, at the expense of the legal entity, in mass media of communication in the area of the practice of the infringement and of the action of the legal entity or, failing that, in publication of the national circulation, as well as by means of visualization of edicts, for a minimum period of 30 (thirty) days, in the establishment itself or in the place of exercise of the activity, in a visible way to the public, and on the website in the global computer network.

§ 6 (VETADO).

Art. 7 The following will be taken into account in the application of sanctions:

I - the seriousness of the infringement;

II - the advantage obtained or intended by the offender;

III - the consummation or not of the infringement;

IV - the degree of injury or danger of injury;

V - the negative effect produced by the infringement;

VI - the economic situation of the offender;

VII - the cooperation of the legal entity for the calculation of infractions;

VIII - the existence of internal mechanisms and procedures of integrity, audit and incentive to report irregularities and the effective application of codes of ethics and conduct in the area of the legal entity;

IX - the value of the contracts maintained by the legal entity with the public body or entity affected; Y

X - (VETADO).

Sole Paragraph. The parameters for evaluating the mechanisms and procedures provided for in section VIII of the caput will be established in the regulations of the federal Executive Power.

CHAPTER IV

OF THE ADMINISTRATIVE PROCEDURE OF RESPONSIBILITY

Art. 8 The establishment and trial of the administrative process for the calculation of the liability of the legal entity correspond to the maximum authority of each body or entity of the Executive, Legislative and Judicial Powers, which will act ex officio or provocation, observing the contradictory and broad defense.

§ 1 ° The competence for the establishment and trial of the administrative process of scrutiny of liability of the legal entity may be delegated, the subdelegation prohibited.

§ 2° In the scope of the federal Executive Power, the Comptroller General of the Union - CGU will have concurrent competence to institute administrative processes of legalization of legal entities or to apply the processes established on the basis of this Law, to examine their regularity or to correct them. progress.

Art. 9 The General Comptroller of the Union - CGU is responsible for the scrutiny, the trial and the trial of the illegal acts foreseen in this Law, practiced against the foreign public administration, observing the provisions of Article 4 of the Convention on Combat. of Corruption of Foreign Public Officials in Commercial Transactions International, promulgated by Decree No. 3,678 of November 30, 2000.

Art. 10. The administrative process for calculating the liability of a legal person will be conducted by a commission appointed by the establishing authority and composed of 2 (two) or more stable servers.

§ 1 ° The public, through its body of judicial representation, or equivalent, at the request of the commission referred to in the caput, may request the necessary judicial measures for the investigation and prosecution of infractions, including search and apprehension.

§ 2 The commission may, with caution, propose to the establishing authority to suspend the effects of the act or process that is the object of the investigation.

§ 3 The commission must conclude the process within a period of 180 (one hundred and eighty) days from the date of publication of the act that institutes it and, at the end, present reports on the established facts and possible liability of the legal entity, suggesting in a motivated way the applicable sanctions.

§ 4° The term provided in § 3o may be extended, through a reasoned act of the establishing authority.

Art. 11. In the administrative process for the calculation of responsibility, the legal entity will be granted a period of 30 (thirty) days for the defense, counted from the citation.

Art. 12. The administrative process, with the report of the commission, will be sent to the establishing authority, in the form of art. 10, for trial.

Art. 13. The establishment of a specific administrative process of integral reparation of the damage does not prejudice the immediate application of the sanctions established in this Law.

Sole Paragraph. Once the process has concluded and there is no payment, the verified credit will be registered in the active debt of the public treasury.

Article 14. Legal personality may be disregarded provided it is used with abuse of the right to facilitate, conceal or disguise the practice of unlawful acts provided for in this Act or to cause patrimonial confusion, being extended all the effects of the sanctions applied to the juridical person to his children administrators and partners with administrative powers, observed the contradictory and the wide defense.

Article 15. The commission appointed to scrutinize the liability of a legal entity, after the conclusion of the administrative procedure, will inform the Public Ministry of its existence, for the examination of possible crimes.

CHAPTER V

OF THE LENVENANCE AGREEMENT

Article 16. The maximum authority of each body or public entity may enter into a leniency agreement with the legal persons responsible for the practice of the acts provided for in this Act that effectively collaborate with the investigations and the administrative process, being that such collaboration result:

I - the identification of others involved in the infringement, when applicable; Y

II - the fast obtaining of information and documents that demonstrate the unlawful under scrutiny.

§ 1 ° The agreement dealt with by the caput can only be concluded if the following requirements are cumulatively met:

I - the legal entity is the first to express its interest in cooperating for the scrutiny of the unlawful act;

II - the legal entity completely ceases its involvement in the investigated infringement from the date of filing the agreement;

III - the legal entity admits its participation in the crime and cooperates fully and permanently with the investigations and the administrative process, sharing, at its expense, whenever it is requested, all the procedural acts, until its closure.

The conclusion of the leniency agreement will exempt the legal entity from the penalties provided in subsection II of art. And in paragraph IV of art. 19 and will reduce by up to 2/3 (two thirds) the value of the applicable fine.

§ 3 The leniency agreement does not exempt the legal entity from the obligation to fully repair the damage caused.

§ 4o O lent agreement will stipulate the necessary conditions to assure the effectiveness of the collaboration or useful result of the process.

§ 5o The effects of accord of leniência will be extended to the legal pessoas that integrates or mesmo economic group, of fato e de direito, since firmm or agreed on set, respected as necces estalelecidas nele.

§ 6o A proposal for agreement of lence will be made public to the effetivation of the respective agreement, unless there is no interest in research and administrative process.

§ 7o It will not matter in the reconnaissance of the illicit act investigated on the basis of a refugee legacy agreement.

§ 8o In the event of failure to comply with the law, a legal entity shall be prevented from entering into a new agreement of 3 (three) years counted as a concession for the public administration of said failure.

§ 9th A celebration of accord of leniência interrompe or prescricional praxis two illicit acts foreseen nesta Lei.

§ 10. A Controladoria-Geral da União - CGU or competent organism to celebrate the accords of leniência not an area of federal Executive Power, as not a case of injurious acts against the public administration estrangeira.

Art. 17. The public administration may also celebrate a legacy agreement with a legal entity responsible for the practice of illicit activities foreseen in Law No. 8,666, of June 21, 1993, commissions for the reduction or reduction of administrative sanctions established in their arts. 86 to 88.

CHAPTER VI

GIVES JUDICIAL RESPONSABILIZATION

1561/5000

§ 4° The leniency agreement will stipulate the necessary conditions to ensure the effectiveness of the collaboration and the useful result of the process.

§ 5o The effects of the leniency agreement will be extended to the legal entities that make up the same economic group, in fact and in law, as long as they sign the agreement as a whole, respecting the conditions established therein.

§ 6 The leniency agreement proposal will only be made public after the effectiveness of the respective agreement, except in the interest of the investigations and the administrative process.

§ 7° It will not matter in recognition of the practice of the illicit act investigated the proposed leniency agreement rejected.

In the case of non-compliance with the leniency agreement, the legal entity will be prevented from entering into a new agreement for a period of 3 (three) years counted as of the knowledge by the public administration of said breach.

§ 9° The conclusion of the leniency agreement interrupts the prescriptive term of the illicit acts foreseen in this Law.

§ 10. The Office of the Comptroller General of the Union - CGU is the competent body to conclude leniency agreements within the scope of the federal Executive Power, as well as in the case of acts harmful to the foreign public administration.

Art. 17. The public administration may also enter into a leniency agreement with the legal entity responsible for the practice of unlawful acts provided for in Law No. 8.666, of June 21, 1993, with a view to the exemption or mitigation of the administrative sanctions established in his arts. 86 to 88.

CHAPTER VI

OF JUDICIAL RESPONSIBILITY

Article 18. In the administrative sphere, the responsibility of the legal entity does not remove the possibility of its responsibility in the judicial sphere.

Art. 19. Because of the practice of acts provided for in art. Within the framework of this Law, the Union, the States, the Federal District and the Municipalities, through the respective Public Advocacies or judicial representation bodies, or equivalent, and the Public Ministry, may judge action with a view to the application of the following sanctions to criminal legal entities:

I - loss of assets, rights or values that represent an advantage or benefit directly or indirectly obtained from the infringement, except the right of the injured party or third party in good faith;

II - suspension or partial interdiction of its activities;

III - mandatory dissolution of the legal entity;

IV - prohibition to receive incentives, subsidies, subsidies, donations or loans from public bodies or entities and public financial institutions or controlled by the public power, for a minimum period of 1 (one) and a maximum of 5 (five) years.

§ 1o The mandatory dissolution of the legal entity will be determined when it is verified:

I - having been the legal personality used on a regular basis to facilitate or promote the practice of unlawful acts; or

II - having been set up to conceal or disguise illicit interests or the identity of the beneficiaries of the acts performed.

§ 2nd (VETADO).

§ 3º Penalties may be applied in isolation or cumulatively.

§ 4º The Public Prosecutor's Office or Public Advocacy or judicial representation body, or equivalent, of the public entity may require the unavailability of goods, rights or values necessary for the guarantee of payment of the fine or of the integral reparation of the damage caused, in accordance with as provided in art. . 7, except the right of the third party in good faith.

Art. 20. In the actions set by the Public Ministry, the sanctions provided for in art. Without prejudice to those foreseen in this Chapter, provided that the omission of the competent authorities to promote administrative responsibility has been verified.

Art. 21. In the actions of judicial responsibility, the rite provided for in Law No. 7,347 of July 24, 1985 will be adopted.

Sole Paragraph. The sentence makes certain the obligation to fully repair the damage caused by the crime, whose value will be found in subsequent liquidation, if not expressly included in the judgment.

CHAPTER VII

FINAL PROVISIONS

Art. 22. The National Cadastral of Punitive Enterprises - CNEP, which will gather and publicize the sanctions applied by the organs or entities of the Executive, Legislative and Judicial Powers of all spheres of government, is created within the scope of the federal Executive Power. based on this Law.

§ lo The bodies and entities referred to in the caput must inform and keep updated, in the Cnep, the data relative to the sanctions applied by them.

§ 2° The Cnep will contain, among others, the following information on the sanctions applied:

I - company name and registration number of the legal person or entity in the National Cadastre of the Legal Entity - CNPJ;

II - type of sanction; Y

III - date of application and final date of the effect of the limiting or impeding effect of the sanction, as the case may be.

§ 3 The competent authorities, in order to conclude leniency agreements provided for in this Law, must also provide and keep updated in the Cnep, after the effectiveness of the respective agreement, the information about the leniency agreement entered into, unless this procedure harms the investigations and the administrative procedure.

§ 4° In the event that the legal entity does not comply with the terms of the leniency agreement, in addition to the information provided in § 3o, reference to the breach must be included in the Cnep.

§ 5° The records of sanctions and leniency agreements will be excluded after the expiration of the term previously established in the sanctioning act or of the full compliance with the leniency agreement and the repair of any damage caused, at the request of the sanctioning body or entity.

Art. 23. The organs or entities of the Executive, Legislative and Judicial Powers of all spheres of government must inform and keep updated, for publicity purposes, in the National Cadastre of Inactive and Suspended Companies - CEIS, of a public nature, instituted in the scope of the federal Executive Power, the data relative to the sanctions applied by them, in the terms of arts. 87 and 88 of Law No. 8.666, of June 21, 1993.

Art. 24. The fine and the loss of property, rights or values applied based on this Law will be destined preferably to the organs or public entities affected.

Art. 25. They prescribe in 5 (five) years the infractions foreseen in this Law, counted from the date of the science of the infraction or, in case of permanent or continuous infraction, of the day in which it has ceased.

Sole Paragraph. In the administrative or judicial sphere, the prescription will be interrupted with the establishment of a process that has as its object the scrutiny of the infraction.

Art. 26. The legal entity will be represented in the administrative process in the form of its statute or social contract.

§ 1o Companies without legal personality will be represented by the person to whom the administration of their assets corresponds.

§ 2° The foreign legal entity will be represented by the manager, representative or administrator of its subsidiary, agency or branch opened or installed in Brazil.

Art. 27. The competent authority that, having knowledge of the infractions foreseen in this Law, does not adopt measures for the scrutiny of the facts will be held criminally, civilly and administratively in accordance with the specific applicable legislation.

Art. 28. This Law applies to acts that are harmful to a Brazilian public entity against foreign public administration, even if committed abroad.

Art. 29. The provisions of this Law do not exclude the powers of the Administrative Council for Economic Defense, the Ministry of Justice and the Ministry of Finance to process and judge an act that constitutes an infringement of the economic order.

Art. 30. The application of the sanctions provided for in this Law does not affect the processes of responsibility and application of penalties derived from:

I - act of administrative improbity under the terms of Law No. 8.429, of June 2, 1992; Y

- II - unlawful acts achieved by Law No. 8.666, of June 21, 1993, or other bidding rules and contracts of the public administration, including in relation to the Differentiated System of Public Procurement - RDC instituted by Law 12.462, of August 4, 1993 2011.

Art. 31. This Law enters into force 180 (one hundred and eighty) days after the date of its publication.

Brasilia, August 1, 2013; 192 of the Independence and 125 of the Republic.

DILMA ROUSSEFF

José Eduardo Cardozo

Luis Inacio Lucena Adams

Jorge Hage Sobrinho"

9.4.1 - Message of the vetoes by the President of Brazil, as an extrajudicial element of interpretation of the law Nº. 12,846 / 2013:

"MESSAGE Nº 314, OF AUGUST 1, 2013.

Mr. President of the Federal Senate,

In the case in question, Of the Constitution, I decided to partially veto, in contrariety to the public interest, the Bill No. 39, of 2013 (No. 6,826 / 10 in the Chamber of Deputies), which "Provides for administrative responsibility and civil of legal persons for the practice of acts against the public administration, national or foreign, and gives other measures".

Hearings, the Ministry of Justice and the Office of the Comptroller General of the Union demonstrated by the veto to the following devices:

§ 6° of art. 6

"§ 6° The value of the fine established in paragraph I of the caput may not exceed the total value of the good or service contracted or provided."

Reasons for the veto

"The device limits to the value of the contract the responsibility of the legal entity that commits illicit acts harmful to the public administration, however, the harmful effects of the crime can be much higher than that value, and other economic advantages derived from it must be considered. Eventual damage to competitors and harm to users.The limitation of the penalty may make it insufficient to effectively punish offenders and discourage future infractions, jeopardizing the effectiveness of the law.

§ 2nd of art. 19

"§ 2nd Depend on the proof of fault or fraud the application of the penalties provided in paragraphs II to IV of the caput of this article."

Reason for the veto

"As expected, the device contrary to the guiding logic of the bill, focusing on the strict liability of legal persons who commit acts against public administration." The introduction of subjective liability will annul all the advances presented by the new law, since there is no mention of the assessment of the culpability of a legal entity.

The Office of the Comptroller General of the Union also opined on the veto of the device described below:

Section X of art. 7

"X - the degree of eventual contribution of public servant behavior for the occurrence of the injurious act."

Reason for the veto

"As proposed, the device unduly equals the participation of the public servant in the act against the administration to the influence of the victim, for the purposes of dosimetry of penalty." There is no sense in assessing the penalty that will be applied to the legal person infringing because of the behavior of the public servant who cooperated for the execution of the act adversely affecting the public administration."

Those, Mr. President, the reasons that led me to veto the aforementioned devices of the project in question, which is subject to the high appreciation of the members of the National Congress."

9.4.2 - Comments on Law no. 12.846 / 2013

We are convinced that the initiative of the National Congress, when enacting Law No. 12,846 / 2013, follows the recommendation that the inter-American anticorruption against corruption causes signatory countries to create effective anti-corruption instruments. the cicc was promulgated in 2002, as follows and it has the following recommendations:

"The President of the Republic, through Decree No. 4,410, of October 7, 2002, promulgates the Inter-American Convention Against Corruption, from which it is extracted that the member states of the Organization of American States are:

"Convinced that corruption undermines the legitimacy of public institutions and attacks society, moral order and justice, as well as against the integral development of peoples;

(...)

Persuaded that the fight against corruption strengthens democratic institutions and avoids distortions in the economy, vices in public management and deterioration of social morality;

recognizing that corruption is often one of the instruments used by organized crime to achieve its ends;

convinced of the importance of generating an awareness among the people of the countries of the region of the existence and seriousness of this problem and of the need to strengthen the participation of civil society in the prevention and fight against corruption, recognizing that corruption in some cases is of international importance, which requires the State to take coordinated action to combat it effectively;

(...)

Deeply concerned at the ever closer links between corruption and revenues from illicit drug trafficking, which threaten and erode legitimate commercial and financial activities and society at all levels;

(...)

determined to make every effort to prevent, detect, punish and eradicate corruption in the exercise of public functions and in acts of corruption specifically linked to their exercise,"

It should be noted that concern about the harmful effects of corruption has won the international forums and that it has been realized that corruption has taken place both in the public sector and in the private sector, which is why a recommendation is made to all countries to take effective measures for their combat.

It is in this context that Law No. 12,846, dated August 1, 2013, effective as of 01/27/2014, authorizes the Power of the Republic to administratively and civilly hold corporations responsible for acts against the public administration, national or foreign, introducing important data such as:

1— objective civil liability;
2— objective administrative accountability;

of the law exsurges that:

1— the legal entity of the private sector as an active subject of administrative or civil wrong;
2— the national or foreign public administration as a taxable person;
3— probity in relations between the private sector and the public sector as a legal object to be protected.

it should be remembered that the liability of the legal entity does not exclude the individual responsibility of its directors or managers or of any natural person, author, co-author or participant in the illegal act, as guaranteed by its art. 3o and also:

1— provides for the liability of the legal entity without excluding the individual responsibility of its directors or managers or any natural person, author, co-author or participant in an illegal act;
2— adopts the monist theory for the contest of people, which determines that Who, in any way, competes for the crime focuses on the penalties to this cominadas, to the extent of their guilt.

in its article 4, it is noted that the law adopts the theory of civil liability for civil damages and considers as acts detrimental to probity in relations with the national and foreign public administration, the following conduct:

1— to promise, offer or give, directly or indirectly, an undue advantage to a public agent, or the third person related to him;
2— prove, finance, fund, sponsor or in any way subsidize the practice of illegal acts provided for in this Law;
3— it is proven that physical or legal persons are used to hide or disguise their real interests or the identity of the beneficiaries of the acts practiced;

in other words, the law creates active administrative corruption (item i), bribery (item ii) and sanctions the use of "oranges or straw men" to conceal the harmful acts of private sector legal entities.

As for the bids and contracts, it repeats the typical criminal figures introduced by Law 8,666 / 1993, articles 89 to 99, as we transcribe to the letter:

"Section III

of crimes and penalties

Art. 89. exempting or not bidding outside the cases provided for by law, or failing to observe the formalities pertinent to the waiver or non-enforceability:

Penalty - detention, from three (3) to five (5) years, and fine.

Single paragraph. The same penalty applies to those who, having proved themselves to be involved in the consummation of the illegal- ity, benefited from the illegal dispensation or unenforceability, in order to conclude a contract with the Government.

Art. 90. To frustrate or defraud, through adjustment, combination or any other expedient, the competitive character of the bidding process, with the purpose of obtaining for itself or for another, an advantage resulting from the award of the object of the bid:

Penalty - detention, from two (2) to four (4) years, and fine.

Art. 91. To sponsor, directly or indirectly, a private interest in the administration, giving rise to the initiation of a license or to the conclusion of a contract, the invalidation of which shall be decreed by the Judiciary:

Penalty - detention, from 6 (six) months to 2 (two) years, and fine.

Art. 92. to admit, enable or cause any modification or advantage, including contractual extension, in favor of the contractor, during the execution of the contracts signed with the Public Authorities, without authorization in law, in the invitation to tender or in the contractual instruments, or, further, pay an invoice with preterity of the chronological order of its enforceability, observing the provisions in art. 121 of this Law: (reda- tion given by Law No. 8,883 of 1994)

Penalty - detention, from two to four years, and fine. (wording given by Law No. 8,883 of 1994)

Single paragraph. the contractor who, having proven to be involved in the achievement of the unlawfulness, obtains an undue advantage or unfairly benefits from the contractual modifications or extensions.

Art. 93. to prevent, disrupt or infringe any act of a tendering procedure:

Penalty - detention, from 6 (six) months to 2 (two) years, and fine.

Art. 94. the confidentiality of a tender submitted in a bidding process, or to provide a third party with the opportunity to dispose of it:

Penalty - detention, from two (2) to three (3) years, and fine.

Art. 95. remove or seek to exclude a bidder by means of violence, serious threat, fraud or offering of an advantage of any kind:

Penalty - detention, from two (2) to four (4) years, and fine, in addition to the penalty corresponding to the violence.

Single paragraph. incurs the same penalty for abstaining or giving up bidding, because of the advantage offered.

Art. 96. To defraud, to the detriment of the Public Treasury, a bid initiated for the acquisition or sale of goods or merchandise, or contract resulting therefrom:

I - arbitrarily raising prices;

II - selling, as true or perfect, falsified or deteriorated merchandise;

III - delivering one commodity for another;

IV - altering the substance, quality or quantity of the goods supplied;

V - rendering, in any way, unjustly, more costly the offer or performance of the contract:

Penalty - detention, from 3 (three) to 6 (six) years, and fine.

Art. 97. admit to bidding or enter into a contract with an enter- prize or professional who has been declared inoperative:

Penalty - detention, from 6 (six) months to 2 (two) years, and fine.

Single paragraph. the same penalty shall be imposed on the person who, declared ini- tially, has tendered or contracted with the administration.

Art. 98. unjustifiably prevent, impede or hinder the registration of any interested party in the registration records or improperly promote the amendment, suspension or cancellation of registration of the registrant:

Penalty - detention, from 6 (six) months to 2 (two) years, and fine.

Art. 99. the penalty of a fine set forth in arts. 89 to 98 of this Law consists in the payment of the amount fixed in the sentence and calculated in percentage indices, whose base will correspond to the value of the advantage actually obtained or potentially obtainable by the agent.

Paragraph 1 - The indices referred to in this article may not be less than 2% (two percent), nor exceed 5% (five percent) of the value of the contract tendered or entered into with exemption or unenforceability of bidding.

Paragraph 2. The proceeds from the collection of the fine shall revert, as the case may be, to the Federal, District, State or Municipal Treasury."

- On the ordinary rite of administrative procedure provided for in Law 12/846/2013

The administrative process for determining the legal entity's responsibility shall be conducted by a commission appointed by the initiating authority and composed of two (2) or more stable servants, and the public entity, through its judicial representation body, or equivalent, at the request of the investigative commission, may request the necessary judicial measures for the investigation and processing of the infractions, including search and seizure.

The proceeding committee may, by way of precautionary measure, petition the initiating authority to suspend the effects of the act or proceeding under investigation and must complete the process within one hundred and eighty (180) days from the date of publication of the act establishing it and, at the end, to present reports on the facts and eventual liability of the legal entity, suggesting in a motivated way the sanctions to be applied.

The term of 180 days admits extension, through a grounded act of the initiating authority.

The legal entity will have a period of 30 (thirty) days for defense, counted from the summons, which must follow the rite determined by Law 9,784 / 1999, by subsidiarity.

The administrative process with the report of the commission shall be sent to the initiating authority, because the instituting and the trial for ascertainment of the responsibility of juridical person rests with the maximum authority of each organ or entity of the Executive, Legislative and Judicial Powers who shall act on his own initiative or by provocation.

The introduction of a specific administrative procedure for full reparation of the damage does not prejudice the immediate application of the sanctions established in the Law, because criminal, civil and administrative liability may be isolated or cumulative.

Once the process has been concluded and there is no payment, the credit calculated will be recorded in the public debt's active debt, that is, by the coordination or recovery services of the active debt of the union in each procurator's office or public entity victimized.

Disregarding the legal entity

Legal personality may be disregarded whenever it is used with abuse of the right to facilitate, cover or disguise the practice of illegal acts provided for by law or to provoke economic confusion, and all effects of the sanctions applied to the legal entity are extended to their administrators and partners with administrative powers, observing the contradictory and ample defense.

Criminal liability

The commission appointed to determine legal entity liability, after the conclusion of the administrative procedure, will inform the Public

Prosecution Office of its existence, in order to determine any crimes. This is because the MP is the ***dominus litis*** of the of art. 129 of cF / 88 and articles 24 to 59 of the Code of Criminal Procedure.

From the leniency agreement

The leniency agreement is nothing more than the preferred disclosure, that is, if the offender delivers effectively, he will receive an award for betraying his accomplices. sign, leniency (from the Latin lenitate) means gentleness, gentleness, sweetness or meekness. In the context of this law, too, it implies a relaxation of the punishment to be imposed.

Finally, it should be noted that the leniency agreement also applies to criminal law in the form of the award award, regulated by Law 9,807 / 99, which establishes rules for the organization and maintenance of special programs for the protection of victims and endangered witnesses, establishes the Federal Assistance Program for Victims and Endangered Witnesses, and provides for the protection of accused or convicted persons who have voluntarily provided effective cooperation in police investigation and criminal prosecution.

Thus, in the event of an act of corruption perpetrated by a legal entity against the national or foreign public administration, the maximum authority of each public body or entity may enter into a leniency agreement with the legal entities responsible for the acts of corruption, when this collaborate effectively with the investigations and the administrative process. effective collaboration is one of which undoubtedly results:

1– the identification of the others involved in the infraction, when applicable;
2– expeditious obtaining of information and documents proving the illicit under investigation.

The leniency agreement may be concluded only if the following requirements are met:

a) the legal entity is the first to express its interest in cooperating to determine the unlawful act;
b) the legal entity completely ceases its involvement in the infraction investigated from the date of the proposal of the agreement;
c) the legal entity admits its participation in the illegal act and cooperates fully and permanently with the investigations and the

administrative process, appearing at its expen- sion whenever requested, to all procedural acts until its closure.

The conclusion of the leniency agreement shall exempt the legal entity from the sanctions provided for in item ii of art. 6 and in section iv of art. 19 and will reduce by two-thirds (two thirds) the applicable fine. however, does not exempt the legal entity from the obligation to make full reparation for the damage caused.

The effects of the leniency agreement shall be extended to legal entities that are part of the same economic group, in fact and in law, provided that they sign the agreement together, respecting the conditions established therein and will only become public after the respective agreement has been reached, except in the interests of investigations and administrative proceedings.

It should be emphasized that the proposal for a rejected lease agreement will not matter in recognition of the practice of the unlawful act investigated. However, in case of breach of the leniency agreement, the legal entity will be prevented from entering into a new agreement for a period of three (3) years as of the knowledge of the public administration of said breach.

Interruption of prescription

The conclusion of the leniency agreement interrupts the prescriptive period of the illicit acts provided for in the Law.

Competence to enter into leniency agreement

The General Controller of the Union - GCU is the competent body to enter into leniency agreements within the Federal Executive Branch, as well as in the case of criminal acts committed against the foreign public administration.

Leniency Agreement under the Law on Bids and Contracts - Law No 8.666 / 1993

The public administration may also enter into a leniency agreement with the legal entity responsible for the practice of illicit activities provided for in Law 8,666 of June 21, 1993, with a view to exempting or mitigating the administrative sanctions established in its articles. 86-88.

Judicial accountability

The responsibility of the legal person in the administrative sphere does not exclude the possibility of its responsibility in the judicial sphere, a hypothesis in which the following sanctions may be applied:

1– forfeiture of assets, rights and values that claim the advantage or benefit directly or indirectly obtained from the infraction, except for the right of the injured party or third party in good faith;

2– suspension or partial prohibition of its activities;

3– compulsory dissolution of the legal entity; and

4– prohibition of receiving incentives, subsidies, grants, donations or loans from public bodies or entities and financial institutions from one to five years.

Compulsory dissolution shall take place if it is established that it has been the legal entity used in a habitual manner to facilitate or promote the practice of illegal acts; and was constituted to conceal or disguise illicit interests or the identity of the beneficiaries of the acts practiced (see article 19)

The competence to request the unavailability of the offender's assets

The Public Prosecutor's Office or the Public Advocate or judicial representation body or equivalent of the public entity may request the unavailability of goods, rights or values necessary to guarantee the payment of the fine or full compensation for the damage caused, as provided in art. 7 of the Law, except for the right of the third party in good faith.

In the actions filed by the Public Prosecutor's Office, the sanctions provided for in art. 6, of the law, provided that the omission of the competent authorities to promote administrative accountability and judicial accountability actions is verified, the rite provided for in Law No. 7,347 of July 24, 1985 shall be adopted.

The conviction renders certain the obligation to make full reparation for the damage caused by the unlawful act, the value of which will be determined upon subsequent liquidation if it is not expressly stated in the judgment.

In the end, it is worth highlighting the fact that the law provides for the creation of a national register of punished companies, which alters them from future legal relations with the national or foreign public administration.

CHAPTER 10

Process System for Legal Assessment of Public Functional Resources in Mercosur

we wish to open this chapter with the study by David Baigun (2006: 37,39) on the efficacy of jus persecuendi and jus puniendi in Argentina, noting that the difficulties are still in Brazil:

"b. La capacidad de persecución de la justicia penal

En la siguiente tabla se presentan datos sobre el estado procesal de los 750 casos almacenados en la base de datos. Los datos corresponden causas que tramitan tanto en el fuero federal como en el ordinario de las diferentes provincias de nuestro país.

Etapas procesal	Causas
etapa de instrucción 439	
tribunal oral 39	
condenas 14	
sentencia 6	
sobreseimiento 84	
sumario 4	

Plenario 20
absolución 2
s/d 142
Total 750

De acuerdo con la información que muestra la tabla, sobre un total de 750, sólo en 14 causas se llegó a una condena definitiva como resultado de la tramitación del proceso penal, mientras que 439 permanecen in etapa de instrucción. (...)

e la siguiente tabla se muestra el estado de la persecución penal para las 239 causas tomadas como muestra en la jurisdicción de la capital del Fuero Federal.

Etapas procesal Causas
etapa de instrucción 112
condenas 7
Plenario 15
sentencia 2
sobreseimiento 84
sumario 3
tribunal oral 16
Total 239

In short, there are too many processes and less results. the principle of the reasonable duration of the proceedings remains always impaired due to factors such as:

1– number of insufficient servers;

2– number of judges insufficient;

3– precarious organic structure of the organs of jurisdiction;

4– existence of unreal or unenforceable laws;

5– existence of real laws, but not applied;

6– existence of excess resources precisely to hinder the application of justice, sometimes by the initiative of the parliamentarians themselves, who, knowing that they can be caught in acts of corruption, seek to protect themselves. in other cases the state itself promotes the enactment of laws that obstruct justice, in order to protect itself when the citizen strikes to his or her capacity by invoking judicial protection;

7– corruption in the judiciary.

10.1 - Specific procedure for the prosecution of crimes of civil servants

From the study of comparative law that we have done in the legislation of the member countries of Mercosur, we realize that only Brazil has a specific procedure for judging the crimes of civil servants.

This is the comparative

ARGENTINA	There is no provision in the Code of Criminal Procedure for the prosecution of crimes of Public Officials' liability.
BRAZIL	Only Brazil has. is provided for in articles 221 and 513 to 518 of the cPP, the procedure for the prosecution of crimes of public officials.
PARAGUAY	There is no provision in the Code of Criminal Procedure for the prosecution of crimes of Public Officials' liability.

URUGUAY	There is no provision in the Code of Criminal Procedure for the prosecution of crimes of Public Officials' liability.
VENEZUELA	There is no provision in the Code of Criminal Procedure for the prosecution of crimes of Public Officials' liability.

The Brazilian Code of Criminal Procedure7 (Decree-Law No. 3,689, October 3, 1941) provides for the prosecution of crimes committed by public officials as follows:

"Art. First, the criminal proceedings shall be governed by this Code throughout the entire Brazilian territory, with the exception of:

i - treaties, conventions and rules of international law;

ii - the constitutional prerogatives of the President of the Republic, of the Ministers of State, in crimes related to those of the President of the Republic, and of the Ministers of the Federal Supreme Court, in crimes of responsibility (Constitution, Articles 86, 89, § 2, and 100); (...)

Art. 513. The crimes of public officials, whose trial and judgment shall be the responsibility of the judges, shall be accompanied by a document or justification that presumes the existence of the offense or a reasoned statement that it is impossible to present any such evidence.

Art. 514. In the case of serious crimes, where the complaint or complaint is in due form, the judge shall order the the notification of the accused, to respond in writing, within a period of fifteen days.

Single paragraph. if the defendant's residence is not known, or if he is outside the jurisdiction of the judge, he will be appointed defender, who will be responsible for presenting the preliminary response.

Art. 515. In the case provided for in the preceding article, during the period granted for the answer, the records shall remain in a notary's office, where they may be examined by the accused or his counsel.

Single paragraph. the answer can be instructed with documents and justifications.

Art. 516. The judge shall reject the com- plaint or denunciation, in a reasoned order, if he is satisfied by the respondent's or his counsel's reply that there is no crime or no action.

Art. 517. The complaint or complaint is received, as described in chapter i of Title X of Book i.

Art. 518. In the criminal instruction and in the other terms of the proceedings, the provisions of chapters i and iii, item i, of this Book shall be observed. (...). Here is the transcription of the indicated articles:

"Art. 351. The initial summons shall be made by warrant, when the defendant is in the territory subject to the jurisdiction of the judge who ordered it.

Art. 353. When the defendant is outside the jurisdiction of the trial court,

Art. 355. The pre-litigation will be returned to the prosecuting judge, regardless of the transfer, after the "fulfillment" has been issued and the summons served by the deprecated judge.

Paragraph 1. It is verified that the defendant is in territory subject to the jurisdiction of another judge, to which the judge deprecates the records for the execution of the proceeding, provided there is time to make the citation.

Paragraph 2 certified by the bailiff that the defendant hides himself or herself from being summoned, the charge will be immediately returned, for the purpose foreseen in art. 362. (...)

Art. 358. The service of the military shall be effected by means of the service of the respective service.

Art. 359. the day appointed for a civil servant to appear in court as an accused shall be notified to him as well as to the head of his apportionment.

Art. 360. If the defendant is arrested, he will be personally summoned. (wording given by Law No. 10,792, December 1, 2003)

Art. 361. If the defendant is not found, he will be summoned by notice, with a period of 15 (fifteen) days.

Art. 362. verifying that the defendant hides himself or herself in order not to be summoned, the bailiff shall certify the occurrence and proceed with the summons with due time, in the manner established in arts. 227 to 229 of Law No. 5,869, dated January 11, 1973 - Code of Civil Procedure. (wording given by Law No. 11,719 of 2008).

Single paragraph. If the accused is not summoned, he shall be appointed as the offender. (included in Law No. 11,719 of 2008).

Art. 363. The proceedings will have completed their training when the defendant was summoned. (wording given by Law No. 11,719 of 2008). (...)

Paragraph 1. If the accused is not found, the appointment shall be made by public notice. (included in Law No. 11,719 of 2008). (...)

Art. 367. The proceeding shall continue without the presence of the accused who, summoned or personally summoned for any act, fails to appear for no good reason or, in case of a change of residence, does not communicate the new address to the court. (wording given by Law No. 9,271, dated April 17, 1996)

Art. 368. The accused being abroad, in a known place, shall be summoned by means of a rotatory letter, suspending the course of the limitation period until its fulfillment. (wording given by Law No. 9,271, dated April 17, 1996)

Art. 369. Quotations that are to be made in foreign legacies shall be effected by letter rogatory. (wording given by Law 9.271, dated 17.4.1996) (...)

Art. 518. In the criminal instruction and in the other terms of the proceedings, the provisions of chapters i and iii, item i, of this Book shall be observed. (...). Here is the transcription of the indicated articles:

"Art. 394. The procedure shall be ordinary or special. (as amended by Law No. 11,719 of 2008).

Paragraph 1. The common procedure shall be ordinary, summary or superordinate: (included in Law No. 11,719 of 2008).

i - ordinary, when it has as its object crime whose maximum sanction is equal to or greater than four (4) years of custodial sentence; (included in Law No. 11,719 of 2008).

ii - summary, when it has as its object a crime whose maximum sanction is less than four (4) years of custodial sentence; (included in Law No. 11,719 of 2008).

iii - sumaríssimo, for criminal offenses of lesser offensive potential, according to the law. (included in Law No. 11,719 of 2008). (...)

Art. 395. The denunciation or complaint will be rejected when: (refusal given by Law No. 11,719 of 2008).

I- is manifestly inept; (included in Law No. 11,719 of 2008).

II - there is no procedural requirement or condition for the prosecution; or (included by Law No. 11,719 of 2008).

III - lacking just cause for the prosecution. (included in Law No. 11,719 of 2008).

Art. 396. In the ordinary and summary proceedings, when a complaint is lodged, the judge, if he does not reject it at the outset, will receive it and order the accused to be summoned in writing within ten) days. (wording given by Law No. 11,719 of 2008).

Single paragraph. In the case of a summons, the term for the defense will begin to flow from the personal appearance of the accused or the defendant. (wording given by Law No. 11,719 of 2008).

Art. 396-a. In the response, the accused may challenge prelim- inaries and plead all that is of interest to his defense, provide documents and justifications, specify the evidence required and list evidence, qualifying them and requesting his summons, when necessary. (included in Law No. 11,719 of 2008). (...)

Art. 397. after compliance with the provisions of art. 396-a, and paragraphs of this code, the judge shall summarily acquit the accused when he finds: (wording given by Law No. 11,719 of 2008).

I - the manifest existence of a cause excluding the illegality of the fact; (included in Law No. 11,719 of 2008).

II - the manifest existence of a cause excluding the culpability of the agent, except for non attributability; (included in Law No. 11,719 of 2008).

III- that the fact narrated evidently does not constitute a crime; or (included by Law No. 11,719 of 2008).

iv - extinguished the agent's punishability. (included in Law No. 11,719 of 2008). (...)

Art. 399. Once the complaint or complaint has been received, the judge shall appoint a day and time for the hearing, ordering the summons of the accused, his or her defense counsel, the Public Prosecutor's Office and, as the case may be, the plaintiff and the assistant. (wording given by Law No. 11,719 of 2008).

Paragraph 1, the accused in custody shall be required to attend the interrogation, and the public authority shall arrange for its presentation. (included in Law No. 11,719 of 2008).

Paragraph 2. The judge who presided over the investigation shall pronounce the judgment. (included in Law No. 11,719 of 2008).

Art. 400. At the trial and trial hearing, to be conducted within a maximum period of 60 (sixty) days, statements shall be made by the offended person, by the testimony of the witnesses and by the defense, in the order, except as provided in art. 222 of this Code, as well as to the clarifications of the experts, the confrontations and the recognition of persons and things, and then the accused is questioned. (wording given by Law No. 11,719 of 2008).

§ 1o, the evidence shall be produced in a single hearing, the judge being entitled to reject those considered irrelevant, impertinent or imminent. (included in Law No. 11,719 of 2008).

Paragraph 2. The clarifications of the experts will depend on the prior request of the parties. (included in Law No. 11,719 of 2008).

Art. 401. In the instruction up to eight (8) witnesses may be questioned by the prosecution and eight (8) by the defense. (as amended by Law No. 11,719 of 2008).

§ 1o In this number do not understand those that do not give commitment and those referred. (included in Law No. 11,719 of 2008).

Paragraph 2. The party may desist from the inquiries of any witnesses listed, except as provided in art. 209 of this code. (included in Law No. 11,719 of 2008).

Art. 402. Once the evidence is produced, at the end of the hearing, the Public Ministry, the plaintiff and the assistant, and then the accused may request actions whose necessity arises from circumstances or facts ascertained in the investigation. (wording given by Law No. 11,719 of 2008).

Art. 403. If no request is made, or if it is rejected, final oral arguments shall be offered for twenty (20) minutes, respectively, by the prosecution and defense, which may be extended by a further ten (10) minutes,. (as amended by Law No. 11,719 of 2008).

(1) where there is more than one accused, the time provided for the defense of each shall be individual. (included in Law No. 11,719 of 2008).

§ 2° to the assistant of the Public Prosecution, after the manifestation of this, will be granted 10 (ten) minutes, extending for the same period the time of manifestation of the defense. (included in Law No. 11,719 of 2008).

Paragraph 3, the judge may, given the complexity of the case or the number of accused, grant the parties a period of five (5) days in succession for the presentation of memorials. In this case, you will have a period of 10 (ten) days to deliver the sentence. (included in Law No. 11,719 of 2008).

Art. 404. Due diligence is considered essential, ex officio or at the request of the party, the hearing will be concluded without the final allegations. (wording given by Law No. 11,719 of 2008).

Single paragraph. the parties shall, within a period of five (5) days, present their final arguments, per memorial, and, within a period of ten (10) days, the judge shall render the judgment. (included in Law No. 11,719 of 2008)."

We can say about the Brazilian procedure:

1– That criminal proceedings shall be carried out throughout the Brazilian territory, with the exception of treaties, conventions and rules of international law;
2– That the constitutional prerogatives of the President of the Republic, the Ministers of State, in crimes related to those of the President of the Republic, and Ministers of the Federal Supreme Court, in the crimes of responsibility, are respected;
3– That crimes of responsibility of public officials shall be vested in judges of law;
4– That in the case of a chargeable crime, if the complaint or complaint is in due form, the judge shall order it and order the accused to be notified in writing within a period of fifteen days;
5– That if the accused's residence is not known, or if he is outside the jurisdiction of the judge, he shall be appointed defender, who will be responsible for presenting the preliminary response;
6– That the judge will reject the complaint or denunciation, in a reasoned order, if he is convinced, by the answer of the accused or his counsel, of the inexistence of the crime or of the lack of action;

7– Once the complaint or complaint has been received, it will be the accused quoted and that the initial summons will be made by warrant, when the defendant is in the territory subject to the jurisdiction of the judge who ordered it;

8– When the defendant is outside the territory of the jurisdiction of the trial court, he will be summoned by means of a letter of formal notice;

9– That the service of the military officer shall be done through the head of the respective military service;

10– That the day appointed for a public official to appear in court, as an accused, shall be so notified to him as to the head of his apportionment;

11– That if the defendant is imprisoned, he will be personally quoted;

12– If the defendant is not found, he or she will be summoned by a public notice, with a period of 15 (fifteen) days or verified that it is hidden so as not to be cited, the bailiff shall certify the occurrence and proceed with the right time and that once the summons has been completed with the right time, if the accused does not appear, he shall be appointed as the offender;

13– That the proceeding shall continue without the presence of the accused who, quoted or summoned personally for any act, fails to appear for no good reason or, in the case change of residence, do not communicate the new address to the court;

14– That when the accused is abroad, in a known place, he will be summoned by means of a letter rogatory, suspending the course of the limitation period until its fulfillment and the citations that are to be made in foreign legacies will be effected by means of a letter rogatory.

It should be noted that the expression, excepting the treaties, conventions and rules of international law, confirms the adoption of the relative sovereignty or relative territoriality adopted by Brazil, which implies that if there is political-juridical will it becomes feasible to unify criminal, procedural legislation criminal and administrative disciplinary issues within the framework of Mercosur.

10.2 - the rules of the Brazilian common procedure

On the common or special procedure and its classification we can draw the following synoptic table:

1– That it will be common or special and that the common procedure will be ordinary, summary or summary:

ORDINARY	SUMMARY	VERY SUM
when it has as its object a crime whose maximum sanction is equal to or greater than four (4) years of custodial sentence.	when it has as its object crime whose maximum penalty is less than four (4) years of private penalty.	for criminal offenses of lesser offensive potential, according to the law.

2– That in the ordinary and brief proceedings, when the complaint or complaint is filed, the judge, if he does not reject it, will receive it and order the accused to be summoned to respond to the accusation in writing;

3– That in the answer the accused may argue for preliminary and plead all that is of interest to his defense and that the response is not presented within the legal time limit, or if the accused, mentioned, does not constitute a defense counsel, the judge will appoint counsel to offer written answer, granting it a hearing for ten (10) days;

4– That the judge should summarily acquit the accused when verifying:

the manifest existence of a cause excluding the illegality of the fact.	the manifest existence of a cause excluding the culpability of the agent, except for non-attributability.	that the fact narrated evidently does not constitute a crime.	extinguished the agent's punishability.

The rules we present can be used as paradigms for Mercosur, with the necessary adaptations to each national legislation.

We note that we defend the extinction of any and all privileged forum in cases of crimes and acts of impropriety against the Mercosur Public Administrations.

The functional independence of any agent can not include crimes or acts of impropriety, as as artfully asserts art. 59 of the constitution of the Republic of Uruguay:

"el funcionario existe para la función y no la función para el funcionario;"

FINAL CONSIDERATIONS ON THE BOOK III

Whether Mercosur will survive or not, this is a response that only the future will give. It is certain that whatever the future model of society the right will be part of it. men will always need the help of the rules for living peacefully and another unshakable certainty of human existence is that corruption will also be present as a disintegrating factor of society.

Law, as a science, has always been a powerful tool for fighting corruption. Regrettably, it has always been manipulated by political forces to be less than the justice expects it to be, but, for all this, it does not cease to be the faithful balance to weigh and judge with justice the offender and to say as God said to the Babylonian general Nebuchadnezzar in the book from Daniel: 5: 27-28:

"You were weighed in the balance, and you were found wanting. Divided was your kingdom ..."

Annex 1 - comments on Bill 5900/2013, which makes corruption a heinous crime.

Bill 5900/2013, approved in the Brazilian Federal Senate, will also be appreciated by the Chamber of Deputies. here is the text:

"Letter no. 1,563 (sf)
Your Excellency Mr Marcio Bittar First Secretary of the Chamber of Deputies
subject: Senate bill to review.
Mr. First Secretary,
Brasilia, on July 4, 2013.

I turn to your excellence, in order to be submitted

From the Chamber of Deputies, pursuant to Art. 65 of the Federal Constitution, Senate Bill No. 204 of 2011, authored by Senator Pedro Taques, included in the attached autographs, which "amends art. Law No. 8,072 of July 25, 1990, to provide for the offenses of embezzlement, concussion, excessive extortion, passive corruption and active corruption, as well as simple homicide and its qualified forms, such as heinous crimes; and amends arts. 312, 316, 317 and 333 of Decree-Law No. 2,848, of December 7, 1940 (Criminal Code), to increase the punishment of the offenses set forth therein."

Regards,

Amends art. Law No. 8,072 of July 25, 1990 (Law on Heinous Crimes), to provide for offenses of petulance, concussion, excessive extortion, passive corruption and active corruption, in addition to simple homicide and its qualified forms, such as heinous crimes; and amends arts. 312, 316, 317 and 333 of Decree-Law No. 2,848, of December 7, 1940 (Criminal Code), to increase the punishment of the offenses set forth therein.

The National Congress decrees:

Art. 1 Art. 1 of Law No. 8,072, of July 25, 1990 (Law of Harmonized Crimes), becomes effective with the following addition of VIII:

"Art. 1st..

VIII - embezzlement (article 312, caput and paragraph 1), concussion and excess of exaction (article 316, caput and §§ 1 and 2), passive corruption (article 317, caput) and active corruption (article 333, caput).

.... "(NR)

(...)

Article 3 Art. 312, 316, 317 and 333 of Decree-Law no. 2,848, of December 7, 1940 (Penal Code), shall be in force with the following wording:

"Peculato

Art. 312...

Penalty - imprisonment, from four (4) to twelve (12) years, and fine. (I.e.

§ 1a-A. The penalty is increased by up to 1/3 (one third) in the event of significant damage caused by a political agent or occupant of an effective State career position.

"Concussion Art. 316..

Penalty - confinement, from four (4) to twelve (12) years, and fine.

Excess of Excise.. ....

§ 2o..

Penalty - imprisonment, from four (4) to twelve (12) years, and fine.

Paragraph 3. The penalty is increased by up to 1/3 (one third) in the event of significant damage caused by a political agent or occupant of an effective position of State career. "(NR)

"Passive Corruption

Art. 317.. Penalty - imprisonment, from four (4) to 12 (twelve) years, and fine. (I.e.

Paragraph 3. The penalty is increased by up to 1/3 (one third) in the event of significant damage caused by a political agent or occupant of an effective position of State career. "(NR)

"Active Corruption

Art. 333.. Penalty - imprisonment, from 4 (four) to 12 (twelve) years, and fine.

§ 1o...

Paragraph 2. The penalty is increased by up to 1/3 (one third) in the event of significant damage caused by a political agent or occupant of an effective position of State career. "(NR)

Article 4 This Law shall enter into force on the date of its publication. Federal Senate, on of 2013.

AUTHOR'S COMMENTS

I have no doubt that if social pressure exists the PL will become an ordinary law to modify the Criminal Code, as part of this policy that increasing the punishment of certain crimes we can curb the crime. moreover, this practice of Brazilian legislation is as old and outdated as the habit of editing laws in large numbers wanting to believe that the existence of law in paper safeguards social and legal dignity. history has already proven that this formula is bankrupt.

It does not mean that typing or qualifying offenses does not help. help, yes! But it is naive to think that it extinguishes the problem or even that it can reduce their practice, at least within acceptable limits.

In Brazil we have anti-corruption laws that, if applied alone or cumulatively, would have fostered a culture of respect for law.

Are examples of good Brazilian anti-corruption laws:

1– Law no. 8.429 / 92, Lc 101/2000 (Fiscal Responsibility Law);
2– Law n. 8.137 / 90 (crimes against taxation;
3– Law no. 12,529 / 2011 (Law that curtails the abuse of the economic power).

These and other laws associated with the Penal Code are enough to minimize the more than 200 million reais a year that are diverted from Brazilian public policies into the pocket of corrupt public officials of the three Powers of this republic that has definitely never been and continues not being of the Brazilian people.

A republic can be understood as the gathering of socially living political animals. this living in society is preserved by law, and if it loses its credibility, it also loses its reason for being. Aristotle states with propriety:

"(...) all things are defined by their functions; and from the moment they lose their character, they can no longer be said to be the same; they are only understood under the same denomination." (in: Aristotle, The Politics, Collective Master Thinkers, scale publisher, 15th ed., p.

If political society is a kind of community living in cities, which in turn is a set of citizens, only good laws can keep the members of that community living in respectful peace. since man is an animal predisposed to conflict in its most diverse spheres, respectful peace, be it spontaneous or produced for fear of reprimand, is attainable at higher levels when there is exemplarity on the part of the one in charge.

In another words, when the government corrupts itself, so too do the people corrupt themselves, in a sort of inverted logic in which the accessory carries with it the principal. behold, in the republic the "whole" is the people, with whom the force is or should be. the problem is that the state model that we have long adopted has made people believe that the force is with the government.

Therefore, we reiterate that it is not by creating laws that make our words or our "false morality" effective, but by enforcing and enforcing such laws. this is one of the reasons that leads me to be pessimistic about the transformation of crimes of corruption such as embezzlement, concussion, excess of exaction, passive corruption and active corruption, in heinous crimes, as a solution for Brazil.

What we really need is to comply with the laws we have created and to end impunity once and for all in the country. to denominate an act of corruption of a heinous crime is just another fallacy of the Brazilian legislature, to which sophist, to deceive the people with the cold and empty letter of another useless law, like so many that we have in the country. it is regrettable that this type of strategy works in countries where the educational process is underdeveloped, as is the case in Mercosur member countries.

American television in the 1990s featured a series called X-file, in which the motto was The truth is out there. the legal truth in our formal democracies is out there. she got lost from the right.

The political classes within Mercosur member countries managed to link the educational process to the idea of a quantity of laws and not to the fulfillment of the justice that must come from it.

Thus, day after day the legislative powers issue new laws and the population, without clarification, continues to believe that the new law will be the new messiah; which will finally fulfill the promise of implementing the social rights promised by the Liberal state or the political candidates in which they voted.

Andre Giroux says that "hell is waiting without hope". For those who know how to recognize the farce of formal democracy (the democracy of promises) installed within Mercosur, hell is a reality.

To conclude the comments in this appendix i, we note that crimes of embezzlement, concussion, excessive extortion, passive corruption and active corruption are codified in the penal code and with the exception of active corruption that is an improper crime, all other crimes are classified as crimes of public officials against public administration.

We have already commented on most of the crimes mentioned and we sincerely believe that calling them hideous will not reduce corruption to acceptable levels because what feeds the force of the corrupt is knowing that impunity prevails, regardless of the amount or quality of the sentence.

By way of example, I transcribe the main characteristics of the heinous crimes, according to Law 8,072 / 1990:

"Art. 2. The heinous crimes, the practice of torture, illicit trafficking in narcotics and related drugs, and terrorism are insusceptible to:

i - amnesty, grace and indult;

ii - bail. (wording given by Law No. 11,464 of 2007)

Paragraph 1. The penalty for crime provided for in this article shall be initially complied with in a closed regime. (wording given by Law No. 11,464 of 2007)

§ 2°, the progression of the regime, in the case of those condemned to the crimes foreseen in this article, will take place after the fulfillment of 2/5 (two fifths) of the sentence, if the grievant is primary, and three fifths), if it recurred. (wording given by Law No. 11,464 of 2007)

Paragraph 3, in the event of a conviction, the judge shall decide whether or not the defendant may appeal in freedom. (wording given by Law No. 11,464 of 2007)

Paragraph 4 - The temporary arrest, on which the Law no. 7.960, dated December 21, 1989, in the crimes foreseen in this article, will have a term of 30 (thirty) days, extendable for the same period in case of extreme and proven necessity. (included in Law No. 11,464 of 2007)

Art. 3. The union shall maintain penal establishments of maximum safety intended to comply with sentences imposed on convicts of high risk, whose permanence at state level jeopardizes public order or safety."

As long as we do not change our culture on the masses of corruption and we revisit the uncontrolled legitimacy we confer on our political-legal institutions, our laws will remain words, nothing more than words ...

BIBLIOGRAPHY

AGOSTINHO, Santo. **Confessions**. translation of j. oliveira santos, s.j., Ambrosio de Pina, s.j. São Paulo: New culture, 2000. (the thinkers).

ALBISTUR, emilio a. La corrupción como pecado social, generadora de estructuras de pecado. centro de investigación y acción social, argentina, año XLv, N. 458, p. 531-533, nov. 1996.

ALCAIN, eduardo Morón. **Cuestiones jusfilosóficas en La Alemania de posguerra**: su actualidad. Buenos aires: abeledo-Perrot, 1998.

ALCALDE, carmen. **La filosofía**. 1. ed. españa: Bruguera, s.a., 1972. (si No).

Alertan por omisión en notificación de hepatitis: uruguay. sin datos lo- cales porque médicos no informan. eL país, Montevideo, ciudades- B3, domingo 17 de mayo de 2009.

ANDRIASOLA, Gabriel. **Delitos de corrupción pública**: análisis de la ley 17.060 de 23 de diciembre de 1998. Montevideo: del foro s.r.L, 1999. (monografías jurídicas 4).

ANGELL, Norman. The great illusion. Sérgio Bath. 1. ed. São Paulo: University of Brasilia, 2002. (classics iPri).

ARÉVALOS, evelio Fernández. Órganos constitucionales del estado: poder legislativo, poder ejecutivo, poder judicial, órganos constitucionales extra- poderes. Paraguay: intercontinental, 2003.

ARGENTINA. (1853). **Constitución de la República Argentina**: sancionada el 1º de mayo de 1853, reformada y concordada por la convencion nacional ad hoc el 25 de septiembre de 1860 y con las reformas de las convenciones de 1866, 1898, 1957 y 1994. available at:< http://www.senado. gov.ar/web/interes/constitucion/preambulo.php.> accessed on: 26.04.2011.

ARGENTINA. **Codigo de etica de la funcion pública**. decreto 41/27-ene-1999, **Publicada en el Boletín Oficial** del 03-feb-1999. Número: 29077. Página: 5. available at:< http://www.infoleg.gov.ar> accessed on: 27.04.2011.

ARGENTINA. **Codigo penal**. Ley 11179/30-sep-1921, **Publicada en el Boletín Oficial** del 03-nov-1921, Número: 8300 Página: 1. available at:< http://www.infoleg.gov.ar> accessed on: 27.04.2011.

ARGENTINA. **Codigo procesal penal**. Ley 23984/21-ago-1991, **Publicada en el Boletín Oficial** del 09-sep-1991. Número: 27215. available at:< http://www.infoleg.gov.ar> accessed on: 27.04.2011.

ARGENTINA. Ley 26.388/ 4 de junio del 2008 (promulgada de hecho el 24 de junio de 2008). delitos de cuello Blanco. available: < http://www. jgm. gov.ar> accessed on: 27.04.2011.

ARGENTINA. Ley Nº 189. codigo contencioso administrativo y tributario de la c.a.B.a. (**Boletín Oficial** No 722- Legislatura de la ciudad autónoma de Buenos aires) available at:< http://boletinoficial.buenosaires.gob.ar> accessed on: 27.04.2011.

ARGENTINA. LeY No 2303/07 - se aprueba el código procesal penal de la ciudad autónoma de Buenos aires. available at:< http://www.buenosa- ires. gov.ar> accessed on: 27.04.2011.

ARGENTINA. LeY No 451/00 - aprueba texto del anexo i, como régimen de faltas de la ciudad de Buenos aires. sustituye denominación del capítulo iv del libro ii, y del art. 47 del código contravencional, B.o. Nº 405. eN eL anexo ii deroga ordenanzas, leyes, decretos y resoluciones normas. available at:< http://www.buenosaires.gov.ar> acesso em: 27.04.2011.

Aristóteles, a Política, - coleção Mestres Pensadores, - editora escala, 15a ed.

AsociacioN de MaGistrados deL uruGuaY, abril 1998 Montevi- deo. **El poder judicial frente a la corrupción.** Montevideo: Liventa papelex s.r.L, 1998.

ARTANA, daniel. Los costos económicos de la corrupción. **Idea**, argentina, p. 91-92, ago. 1998.

Autoridades del clínicas cerraron la emergencia por falta de recursos: trasla- dos. Los pacientes son derivados hacia otros centros. eL país, Montevideo, Nacional – a5, domingo 17 de mayo de 2009.

BACON, Francis. Novum organum or true indications about the interpretation of nature. translation and notes of Joseph aluysio reis de andrade. São Paulo: New culture, 2000. (the thinkers).

BAIGUN, david; rivas, Nicolás García (dir.). **Delincuencia económica y corrupción.** 1. ed. Buenos aires: ediar, 2006.

BAKUNIN, Michael alexandrovich. Anarchist texts. translation of Zilá Bernd. selection and notes daniel Guérin. Porto Alegre: L & PM, 2006. (L & PM Pocket Collection).

Baratta, alessandro. Principles of minimum criminal law: for a theory of human rights as the object and limit of criminal law. translation of Francisco Bissoli Filho. published in the journal "Criminal doctrine n. 10-40. Buenos Aires: depalma, 1987. santa catarina, 2003.

BarBoZa, julio. **Derecho Internacional Público.** Buenos aires: Za- valia,1999.

Barrio, javier delgado; viGo, rodolfo L. About legal principles. Buenos aires: abeledo-Perrot. 1998

BeristaiN, antonio. New criminology: the light of direct criminal and victimology. translation of Candido Furtado Mayan Neto. Brasília: University of Brasília, 2000.

BerLiNGer, Giovanni; GarraFa, volnei. The human market: a bioethical study of buying and selling body parts. translations of isabel regina augusto Brasília: University of Brasília, 1996.

Biblia. espanhol. **Santa Biblia.** versión de casiodoro de reina. Madrid: so- ciedad bíblica, 1995.

Brazil. UN. board of financial activities. Money laundering: a worldwide problem. Brasília: UNDP, 1999.

BoBBio, Norberto. Theory of legal order. translation of Maria celeste lamb Milk of the saints. 10. ed. Brasília: University of Brasília, 1999.

Brazil. Federal Court of Justice. Meetings of Supreme Courts: Challenges and Perspectives in the Mercosur Integration Process. Brasília: Supreme Court Forum, 2007.

CaLdWeLL, Taylor. An iron pillar. translation of Luzia Machado da Costa. rio de janeiro: record distributor of press services s.a., 1965.

CarBoNeLL, Miguel; saLaZar, Pedro (eds.). **Garantismo**: estudios so- bre el pensamiento jurídico de Luigi Ferrajoli. Madrid: trota, 2005. (colec- ción estructuras y procesos serie derecho).

Castro, anna Maria; days, edmundo F. Introduction to social thought. 4. ed. rio de janeiro: eldorado, 1976.

CateNacci, imerio jorge. **Introducción al derecho**: teoría general. ar- gumentación razonamiento jurídico. 1. ed. Buenos aires: astrea, 2006. v. 1. reimpresión. (colección mayor Filosofía y derecho v. 7).

Chaui, Marilena. What is ideology. 26. ed. São Paulo: publisher brasiliense, 1988. (First 13 steps).

ChoMsKY, Noam. Reasons for status. translations of vera ribeiro. record.

ChurchiLL, Winston s. Memories of World War II. translations of vera ribeiro. 2. ed. Rio de Janeiro: New Frontier, 1995. v. 7. Printing.

CicerÓN. Los oficios. traducción Manuel de valbuena. Madrid: espasa. (Grandes clásicos universales).

CiNcuNeGui, juan Bautista; ciNcuNeGui, juan de dios. **La corrupción y los factores de poder.** 1. ed. argentina: Fundación argentina de planeamiento, 1996.

CoLeGio de coNtadores Y ecoNoMistas deL uruGuaY. **"Cambios en la administración financiera gubernamental".** Montevideo: colegio de contadores y economistas del uruguay. 1999.

CoMissiÓN de seGuiMeNto deL cuMPLiMieNto de La coN- veNciÓN iNteraMericaNa coNtra La corruPciÓN. colegio público de abogados de la capital federal. Buenos aires, 2002.

CoMisiÓN ecoNÓMica Para aMÉrica LatiNa Y eL cariBe. **Balance preliminar de las economías de América latia y el Carbe.** chile: Naciones unidas, 2008.

CoMisiÓN ecoNÓMica Para aMÉrica LatiNa Y eL cariBe. **Es- tudio económico de América latina y el Caribe:** política macroeconómica y volatilidad. chile: Naciones unidas, 2008.

CoMte, auguste. curso de filosofia positiva. traducción de carmen Lessining. 1. ed. Buenos aires: Need, 2004. (ediciones libertador).

CoNsejo de La MaGistratura Poder judiciaL de La ciudad de BueNos aires. La planificación estratégica en la justicia de la ciudad de Buenos aires. argentina: Geudeba, 2008.

CoNveNciÓN de NacioNes uNidas coNtra La corruPciÓN : Nuevos paradigmas para la prevención y combate de la corrupción en el escenario global. 1. ed. Buenos aires: oficina anticorrupción. Ministerio de justicia y derechos humanos, 2004.

Corrupción y democracia en la argentina: La interpretación de los estudiantes universitarios. **Revista Argentina de sociología.** argentina, año 3, N°4, p. 9-31, 2005.

Coast, josé armando. Legal outline of administrative improbity. Brasília: Legal Brasília, 2000.

CouLaNGes, Fustel de. The ancient city: studies on worship, law, the institutions of Greece and Rome. translation of jonas camargo Leite and eduardo Fonseca. São Paulo: hemus, 1975.

CreteLLa juNior, josé. Course of Roman law. 1. ed. rio de janeiro: forensic, 1968.

Christianity, Fortini. et al. (org.). Public policies: possibilities and limits. Belo Horizonte: Forum, 2008.

Croce, Benedetto. et al. Declarations of rights. Brasília: Project Foundation rondon, 1988.

DarWiN, charles. **El origen de las espécies**. 1. ed. Buenos aires: centro editor de cultura, 2006.

DeLMas-MartY, Mireille. Three challenges for a world right. translation and afterword of Fauzi hassan choukr. Rio de Janeiro: Lumen juris, 2003.

Protection and Economics Division of the Ministry of Economic Law of the Ministry of

Justice. Combat cartels and leniency programs. Brasília: official publication, 2008. (sde / dPde 01/2008).

Discards. Discourse of method, the passions of the soul, meditations. São Paulo: New culture, 2000. (the thinkers).

Aspects of sovereignty in international law: it addresses the internal and external aspects of sovereignty, analyzing the subsistence of sovereignty in the process of integration found at the international level. available at: <http://www.direitonet.com.br/artigos/exibir/1496/aspectos-so-sovereign-international-record>. access on: 03.06.2011.

Eco, Umberto. **Como se hace una tesis**: técnicas y procedimientos de investigación, estudio y escritura. Barcelona: editora Gedisa, s.a., 1988.

EL Poder judiciaL aNte La corruPciÓN. cuaderno No 2, 2004, Montevideo. ¿Qué justicia queremos? Uruguay: asociación de funcionarios judiciales del Uruguay, 2004. 32 p.

ENGeLs, Friedrich. The origin of the family, private property and the State. translation ciro Mioranza. São Paulo: scale. (Great works of universal thought - 2).

EtKiN, jorge ricardo. La doble moral de las organizaciones: los sistemas perversos y La corrupción institucionalizada. españa: McGraW-hiLL, 1993. p. 266.

FerMíN, claudio. **100 razones para salir de Chávez**. venezuela: democracia y periodismo, 2004.

FerNaNdes, a.; GaveGLio, s.(comp.). **Globalización, integración, Mercosur y desarrollo local**. 1. ed. argentina: homo sapiens ediciones, 2000.

Foro uNiÓN euroPea, aMÉrica LatiNa Y eL cariBe Las PoLíticas FiscaLes eN tieMPos de crisis: voLatiLidad, co- hesiÓN sociaL Y ecoNoMía PoLítica de Las reForMas. 2009, Montevideo. **El papel de la política tributaria frente a la crisis global**: con- secuencias y perspectivas. Montevideo: Naciones unidas, 2009. 48p.

Foro uNiÓN euroPea, aMÉrica LatiNa Y eL cariBe Las PoLíticas FiscaLes eN tieMPos de crisis: voLatiLidad, co- hesiÓN sociaL Y ecoNoMía PoLítica de Las reForMas. 2009,

Montevideo. **Crisis, volatilidad, ciclo y política fiscal en América latina**. Montevideo: Naciones unidas, 2009. 44 p.

GaLes casa caMBiaria LesPaN s. a. **Manual de prevención de la- vado de activos**. Montevideo- uruguay: Gales casa cambiaria lespan s. a., 2004. 119 p.

GaLvão, eduardo rodrigues. Study of Brazilian problems. 3. ed. Brasília: Federal senate, graphic center, 1985.

GiLes, Thomas ransom. History of education. São Paulo: ePu, 1987.

GoMÁ, javier. **Ejemplaridad pública**. 2. ed. Madrid: taurus pensamiento,

2009.

GoMes, Luis roberto. Public ministry and control of administrative omission: control of state omission in environmental law. 1. ed. Rio de Janeiro: University Forensics, 2003.

GroNdoNa, Mariano. **La corrupción**. 3. ed. argentina: editorial planeta argentina, 1993.

Guedes, jefferson cárus; Souza, Luciane Moessa (coord.). State Advocacy: institutional issues for the construction of a state of justice: studies in homage to Figueiredo Moreira Neto and José Antonio toffoli days. Belo Horizonte: Forum, 2009.

HeideMaNN, Francisco; SaLM, Jose Francisco (org.). Public policies and development: epistemological bases and models of analysis. 2. ed. Brasília: University of Brasília, 2010.

HesPaNha, antónio Manuel. European legal culture: synthesis of a millennium. Florianópolis: Boiteux Foundation, 2005.

Hooter The Odyssey. translation and adaptation Fernando c. of Araújo Gomes. São Paulo: scale. (Master thinkers).

Hume. São Paulo: New culture, 2000. (the thinkers).

JacKsoN, Philip W., et al. **La vida moral en la escuela**. traducción de Glória vitale. Buenos aires: amorrortu, 2003.

JiMÉNeZ, juan Pablo; PodestÁ, andrea. **Inversión, incentivos fiscales y gastos tributarios en América latina.** santiago de chile: Naciones unidas, 2009. (serie macroeconomía del desarrollo).

JuNta asesora eN Materia ecoNÓMico FiNaNceira deL es- tado. Ética y función pública. 1. ed. Montevideo: tarma, 2008. 60 p. (se- rie: "manuales de capacitación" no 1).

JuNta asesora eN Materia ecoNÓMico FiNaNceira deL es- tado. **Normas de conduta en la función pública.** Montevideo: tarma, 2007.

KaFKa, Franz. **Consideraciones acerca del pecado**: cuadernos en octava. Buenos aires: ediciones libertador, 2004. (edición especial).

KaFKa, Franz. The process. São Paulo: Martin claret, 2000. (the masterpiece of each author).

KaNt, immanuel. Critique of pure reason. translation of valerio rohden and udo Baldur Moosburger. São Paulo: New culture, 2000. (the thinkers).

KaNeNGuiser, Nartín. **Elfin de La ilusión**: argentina 2001·2011 crisis, reconstrucción y declive. 1. ed. Buenos aires: edhasa, 2011.

KLuG, ulrich. Legal logic. translation of j. c Gardella. Bogotá: temis, 2004. v. 2. reprint

KNeLLer, George F. Science as a human activity. translation of antonio josé de souza. Rio de Janeiro: Zahar, 1980.La Lucha MuNdiaL coNtra La corruPcióN. Foro Politico: re- vista del instituto de ciencias Politicas. v.Xvi Buenos aires: universidad del Museo social argentino, Marzo 1996. p. 76-81.

LaNdes, david s. Wealth and the poverty of nations: why some are so rich and others are so poor. 2. ed. translation of Álvaro Cabra. Rio de Janeiro: campus, 1998.

LeNaY, charles. **La evolución**: de La bactéria al hombre. traducción y adaptación Pilar Martinez. Barcelona: rBa, 1994. (conocer la ciencia).

Levi, josé Fernando casañas. **Legislación penal Paraguaya**: código penal concordado, código procesal penal concordado, leyes complementares, acordadas y resoluciones de la corte suprema de justicia, resoluciones del ministerios público, índice alfabético. Paraguay: intercontinental, 2006. (legislación Paraguaya edición 2006).

LocKe, john. Essay on human understanding. translations of anoar aiex. São Paulo: New culture, 2000. (the thinkers).

LocKe, john. Second Treatise about Government. translation of alex Marins. São Paulo: Martin Claret, 2002. (the masterpiece of each author)

LoNG, Kim. The almanac of political corruption, scandals & dirty politics. New York: Delacorte Press, 2007.

MahiQues, carlos alberto (dir.). el derecho penal: doctrina y jurisprudencia. Buenos aires: el derecho, 2005. p. 6

MairaL, héctor a., **Las raíces legales de la corrupción**: o de cómo el derecho público fomenta la corrupción en lugar de combatirla. 1. ed. argentina: ediciones rap s.a, 2007.

MaLMesBurY, Thomas hobbes. Leviathan or matter, form and power of an ecclesiastical and civil State. translation of joão Paulo Monteiro and Maria Beatriz Nizza da silva. São Paulo: New culture, 2000. (the thinkers).

MaNcuso, hugo r. Methodology of research in social sciences: theoretical and practical guidelines of semioepistemology. 1. ed. Good air: Paidós, 2006. 3. v. reprint.

MaNcuso, Rodolfo de Camargo. Public civil action: in defense of the environment, cultural heritage and consumers. 8. ed. Brazil: journal of the courts, 2002.

MaNFroNi, carlos a. **La convención interamericana contra la corrupción**. 2. ed. argentina: abeledo-Perrot, 2001.

MaNFroNi, carlos a. **Soborno transnacional**. 1. ed. argentina: abele- do-Perrot, 1998.

Manual on monitoring of alternative penalties and measures. Brazil: pan-fler Graph, 2002.

MartiNo, antonio a. etica y democracia. Foro Politico: revista del in- stituto de ciencias Politicas. v.Xii. Buenos aires: universidad del Museo social argentino, diciembre 1994. p. 7-10.

MeNdieta, Manuel villoria. Ética pública y corrupción: curso de ética administrativa. 1. ed. Madrid: editorial tecnos grupo anaya s.a., 2000.

MeNY, Yves; thoeNiG, jean-claude. **Las políticas públicas**. versión es-pañola Francisco Morata. traducción de salvador del carril. 1. ed. Barce-lona: ariel ciencia política, 1992.

MiNisterio de justicia Y derechos huMaNos: balance de ges- tion; oficina anticorrupcion. argentina, 2000. p. 49

MiNisterio FederaL de cooPeraciÓN ecoNoMica Y desar- roLLo. **Carpeta de información:** la cooperación alemana para el desar- rollo con américa latina y el caribe. Berlim, 2005.

MoNtesQuieu. Of the spirit of the laws. v. 1. Sao Paulo: New culture, 2000. (the thinkers).

MoNti, víctor Manuel. **Corrupción, gobierno y democracia**. ricardo G. herrera (col) 1. ed. santiago del estero: uNca, 1999.

Moreira Neto, Diogo of Figueredo. Four paradigms of postmodern administrative law: legitimacy, purpose, efficiency, results. Belo Horizonte: Forum, 2008.

Moro, tomas. *Utopia*. traducción María Guillermina Nicolini. Buenos aires: editorial La Página s.a. editorial Losada s.a. 2003.

NeuMaNN, ulfried. **La pretensión de verdad en el derecho**: y três ensay-os sobre radbruch. traducción Mauricio hernández. 1. ed. colombia: universidad externado de colombia, 2006. (serie de teoria jurídica y filosofia del derecho n 38).

NietZsche, Friedrich. **Así habló Zaratustra**. traducción por j. c García Borrón. 1. ed. Buenos aires: centro editor de cultura, 2007.

NietZsche, Friedrich. **La genealogía de la moral**. traducción por ser- gio albano. 1. ed. Buenos aires: Gradifco, 2007. (Pensadores universales).

NietZsche, Friedrich. **Más allá del bien y del mal**. traducción por sergio albano. 1. ed. caseros: Gradifco, 2007. (Pensadores universales).

NiNo, carlos santiago. Ética y derechos humanos: un ensayo de funda-mentación. 2. ed. Buenos aires: astrea, 2007. v. 2. reimpresión. (colección mayor Filosofía y derecho v. 15).

NÚÑeZ, josé ariel. **Manual de auditoría gubernamental**: control democrático contra La corrupción y el despilfarro. Buenos aires: edi-ciones rap,2006.

OLivÉ, juan carlos Ferré. et al. **Blanqueo de dinero y corrupción en el sistema bancario**: delitos financieros, fraude y corrupción en europa. v. ii. españa: universidad de salamanca, 2002.

OLiveira, harrison. Reflections on the misery of the northeast. Paraíba: "the union" cia. publisher, 1984.

OLiveira, odete Maria. Prison: a social paradox. 3. ed. santa cata- rina: ed. of uFsc, 2003.

OLiveira, roberto cardoso; BaiNes, stephen G. (org.). Nationality and ethnicity at borders. Brasília: University of Brasília, 2005. (collection americas).PaLacio, ernesto. **Catilina**: una revolución contra la plutocracia en roma. Buenos aires: abeledo-Perrot, 1998.

LA PaLoMBara, Joseph. Politics within the nations. Brasília: university of Brasília, 1982. (Political thought 60).

ParaGuaY. constitución (1992). **Constitución de la república del Para-guay:** promulgación 16 de agosto de 1992. elaborado por horacio antonio pettit. Paraguay: intercontinental, 2008.(tomo iv libro noveno).

Passet, Rene. The neoliberal illusion. translation of clóvis Marques. record.

Patel, Ketan et al. The master of strategy: power, purpose and principle. translation of ricardo doninelli. Rio de Janeiro: Bestseller, 2007.

PeGoraro, juan s. La corrupción como cuestión social y como cuestión penal. delito y sociedad, Buenos aires, año 8, n.13, p. 6-32, 1999.

Pereira juNior, jessé torres. The right to defense in the 1998 constitution: the administrative procedure and the accused in general. rio de janeiro: renovar, 1991.

Porto, Maria stela Grossi; dWYer, tom (org.). Sociology and reality: social research in the XXI century. Brasília: University of Brasília, 2006.

PritZL, rupert: corrupción y rentismo en américa Latina. Buenos aires: ciedla, Fundación honrad adenauer, 2000.

ProGraMa de cooPeraciÓN cePaL- GtZ. Memoria anual marzo 2007-marzo 2008. santiago de chile: Naciones unidas, 2007-2008.

Puerto, carlos Gonzalez del; MÓdica, Yeny villalba y Gisela di (comp.). **Compilación legislativa en materia de prevención y lucha contra la corrupción**. Paraguay: Publicación del instituto de estudios en ciencias penales y sociales del Paraguay (inecip), 2004.

QuiNta cuMBre de Las aMericas. 5. 2009, Puerto españa. **La reac- ción de los gobiernos de las Américas frente a la crisis internacional:** una presentación sintética de las medidas de política anunciadas hasta el 31 de marzo de 2009. santiago de chile: Naciones unidas, 2009. 57 p.

RaBiNovich – BerKMaN, ricardo david. **Derechos humanos**: uma introducción a su naturaleza y a su historia. 1. ed. Buenos aires: Quorum, 2007.

RaBiNovich – BerKMaN, ricardo david. **Principios generales del derecho latinoamericano**. Buenos aires: astrea, 2006.

RaBiNovich – BerKMaN, ricardo david. **Un viaje por la historia del derecho**. 1. ed. Buenos aires: Quorum, 2007.

REIS, claudio araujo. Unity & freedom: the individual according to jean-jacques rousseau. Brasília: University of Brasília: Fi- natec, 2005.

ReLatorio da cia: how will the world in 2010. translation of claudio Blanc and Marly Netto Peres. São Paulo: editor, 2006.

RePuBLica deL ParaGuaY. **Manual de procedimientos estadísticas penales antecedentes judiciales**. Paraguay, 2007.

RePÚBLica orieNtaL deL uruGuaY. **Ley de fortalecimiento del sistema de prevención y control del lavado de activos y financiación del terrorismo**: ley no 17.835 del 23/09/004. uruguay: direccion nacional de impresiones y publicaciones oficiales. 2004.

RIMONDI, jorge Luis. **Calificación legal de los actos de corrupción en La administración pública**. 1. ed. Buenos aires: ad- hoc, 2005.

ROJAS, ricardo M. algunas consideraciones filosófico-políticas en torno al problema de la corrupción. Foro Politico: revista del instituto de ciencias Politicas. v. vii. Buenos aires: universidad del Museo social argentino, abril 1993. p. 61-82.

RUGNITZ, josé. **La polibanda**. Montevideo: La republica, 2002. (caso clave: temas de investigación de la república).

Sounds, Jerônimo jesus. Conduct adjustment Term. 1. ed. Rio de Janeiro: publisher and legal bookstore of Rio de Janeiro, 2005.

Plama rude. How to fight corruption. São Paulo: Paullus, 2009.

SCHIJMAN, jorGe horacio. **La Justicia en los procesos de inte- gración**. *Conceptos - Boletín de la Universidad del Museo Social Argen- tino,* argentina, ciencias jurídicas, p. 5, aÑo 81 – enero – diciembre 2006.

SCHIMITT, carl. Political theology. translation of elisete antoniuk. Belo horizonte: del rey, 2006.

SCHOPENHAUER, arthur. **Ensayo sobre al libre albedrío:** la libertad. traducción por sergio albano. Buenos aires: Gradifco, 2006. (Pensadores universales).

SIGMUND, Freud. **Obras completas**. traducción por Luis Lopez. v. 2. Ma- drid: biblioteca nueva Madrid, 1968.

SILVA, Nelson Lehmann. The civil religion of the modern state. Brasília: Thesaurus, 1985.

SKINNER, Quentin. The foundations of modern political thought. renato janine ribeiro and Laura texeira Motta. São Paulo: company of letters, 2006. v. 4. reprint.

SMITH, adam. **Vida, pensamiento y obra**. españa (colección grandes pen- sadores).1997.

SOUZA, jessé (org.). Democracy today: new challenges for contemporary democratic theory. 1. ed. Brazil: University of Brasília, 2001.

SPINOZA, Baruch de. Ethics: demonstrated in the manner of geometers. São Paulo: Martin Claret, 2002. (the masterpiece of each author)

SUPIOT, alain. **Homo juridicus**: ensayo sobre La función antropológica del derecho. traducción de silvio Mattoni. 1. ed. Buenos aires: siglo vein- tiuno editores, 2007 (sociología y política).

TEIXEIRA, joão Gabriel Lima (coord.). The construction of citizenship. Brasília: University of Brasília, 1986.

TOCQUEVILLE, alexis de. **La democracia en América**. traducción de Luis r. cuéllar. 2. ed. México: Fondo de cultura económica, 1957.13.v. reimpresión.

TODARELLO, Guillermo ariel. corrupción administrativa y enriquecimiento ilícito. 1. ed. Buenos aires: del Puerto, 2008.

TRIGUERO, andré. Sustainable world 2: new directions for a planet in crisis. São Paulo: Globo, 2012

TRINDADE, antonio augusto cançado. The exhaustion of internal resources in international law. 2. ed. Brasília: publisher of Brasília, 1997.

VAINER, ari, et al. Responsible municipal tax management: annual budget law. Brasília: Area of communication and culture-executive marketing management, 2001.

VAINER, ari, et al. Responsible municipal tax management simple: multi-year manual drafting. Brasília: Area of communication and culture-executive marketing management, 2001.

VAINER, ari, et al. Responsible municipal tax management simple: budget guidelines manual drafting manual. Brasília: Area of communication and culture-executive marketing management, 2001.

VÁZQUEZ, Mariana Malet. **La corrupción en la administración pública**: aproximación a la ley no 17.060 normas referidas al uso indebido del poder público. Montevideo: carlos alvarez. 1999.

VIDAL, j. W. Baptist. From servile state to sovereign nation: solidarity civilization of the tropics. Petrópolis: voices, 1987.

VIGO, rodolfo Luis. **De la ley al derecho**. 2. ed. México: Porrúa, 2005.

VIGO, rodolfo Luis. **La injusticia extrema nos ES derecho**. 1. ed. Buenos aires: La Ley: universidad de Buenos aires.Faculdade de derecho, 2006. 1. v. reimpresión

VIGO, rodolfo Luis. **Perspectivas iusfilosóficas contemporâneas**: ross, hart, Bobbio, dworkin, villey, alexy, Finnis. 2. ed. Buenos aires: abeledo-Perrot, 2006.

VIRGOLINI, julio e.s. crímenes excelentes: delitos de cuello blanco, crimen organizado y corrupción. Buenos aires: del Puerto, 2004. (colección tesis doctoral 2).

VOLTAIRE. **Cartas filosóficas**. traducción y notas Fernando savater. Barcelona: altaya, 1993. (Grandes obras del pensamiento v. 7).